Dogs and Ladies
Not Allowed

The 200 Year History
of Liverpool Cricket Club

1807 - 2007

**Written and compiled by
Tony Onslow and John Sturgeon**

First Published 2007 by Countyvise Limited,
14 Appin Road, Birkenhead, Wirral CH41 9HH.

British Library Cataloguing in Publication Data.
A catalogue record for this book is available from the British Library.

ISBN 978 1901231 84 7

Acknowledgements

The following people have rendered invaluable assistance during the research that was required to produce this book and without them the task could not have been completed.

Don Ambrose, David Blackmore Gill Cussons, Pat Broome, Dick Daglish, Peter Hall, David Gillooley, Rev Malcolm Lorimar, Chris Jones, Rev Malcolm Lorimar, Janet McMullin, Alan Newton, Sue Newton M.B.E, Ruth Sturgeon, Ray Tyler, Eric Ward, Jean Ward and John Weare, We would also like to acknowledge the contribution made by all the staff at the Local Record Library, Liverpool Central Library.

Foreword

'Dogs and Ladies Not Allowed: The 200 Year History of Liverpool Cricket Club' is one of two approaches being made to reclaim the history of the Club. This research and historical narrative is one, and the gathering together, renovation, organisation and secure storing of the written records and historical photographs of the Club for future reference is the second. During years of neglect, important archive items had been allowed to disappear or degenerate. But, with this carefully researched historical account and restoration of the records, historical interest in the background of the Club and its relationship to the developments of the City will have been enhanced. This Heritage Project has been in the hands of two Club members, Tony Onslow and John Sturgeon. They have demonstrated great skill and commitment as Honorary Club Historian and Honorary Club Archivist. The Club would be delighted for Club members to pass on archive items for safe keeping which might contribute to the growing stock of material being catalogued.

Circumstantial evidence clearly links the Aigburth Club with the Mosslake Fields Cricket Society of 1807 and the Liverpool merchant gentlemen's sporting sub-culture of the time. From the 1880s detailed records of the Club's committees have been the source of information; whilst for more recent times the accounts of long serving members have supplied living detail. Not only cricket, which is the spiritual heart and physical structure of the Aigburth Club, but other sporting sections also demonstrate important involvement with elite sporting activities in the North of England in the late 18th Century e.g. rugby, tennis and hockey. The Club style has developed from the Liverpool patrician families, public school influenced values, as the title of the book illustrates: 'Dogs and Ladies Not Allowed Beyond This Notice', which was still on display on the steps to the pavilion in the 1960s.

It is fortuitous that the bicentenary of the Club leads into the opening of Liverpool's City of Culture Year 2008. Sporting culture will feature prominently in that celebration and the long established connections of all the different participatory sports flourishing under the banner of Liverpool Cricket Club relate very importantly to this City event and achievement. This historical account clearly demonstrates the influence of Liverpool City developments on the progress of Liverpool Cricket Club.

The aim of the writers of this history is to present a story of this long established sporting institution, which is interesting and enjoyable. It can also be seen as being a road map from the Club's roots to the Bicentenary Celebration: a reminder to current members of this influential heritage. Great sporting attainment has been achieved at Aigburth by accomplished players in a number of sports in the past and the theme of the bicentenary celebration is to ensure that this continues.

Please read and enjoy 'Dogs and Ladies Not Allowed', and appreciate the contribution of its creators Tony Onslow and John Sturgeon.

Eric Ward, Liverpool Cricket Club President 2005-2007

The 4th Earl of Sefton

President 1881 - 1897

CHAPTER 1

The Advent
of Cricket in Lancashire

The present day Liverpool Cricket Ground at Aigburth was opened in 1881. The idyllic location is dominated by a three storey pavilion that was, at the time of its inauguration, the finest in England. This imposing red brick structure looks out proudly over an excellent playing field and on to the line of tennis courts that are positioned to the rear of the far sight screen. The visiting players, while sitting on the top balcony, are rewarded with a clear view across the broad expanse of the River Mersey. This most agreeable aspect is further enhanced by the placid backdrop provided by the dark outline of the Clwyd Hills. This pleasant venue is a tribute to the proud and self confident people of Victorian Liverpool who, in 1807, first brought cricket to the Red Rose County.

Although there is no proof to validate the fact, it is probable that the game of cricket was introduced to Liverpool by Banastre Tarleton. His forefathers were a successful family of Liverpool Merchants who were first reported to be living in Aigburth during the 13th century.

Born on 21st August 1754, Banastre Tarleton studied law at Oxford before enlisting to fight in the American War of Independence. His daring exploits during the conflict, saw him promoted to Colonel before he arrived back in London to be awarded celebrity status. He quickly settled into London society where, despite the loss of two fingers, he earned a reputation for his ability on the cricket field.

The London press was quick to acknowledge his skills and mentioned him as being one of the better players. ... *"The Prince of Wales and a great number of Nobility and foreigners of distinction were present. Lord Winchilsea the best bat, Col Tarleton the best bowler."*(General Evening Post May 22nd 1784.) *"A grand cricket match was played at the White Conduit Fields. Amongst the players present were: The Duke of Dorset, Lord Winchilsea, Lord Talbot and Col Tarleton. A pavilion was erected for refreshments, and a number of Ladies attended."* ... (London Chronicle 29 May 1784.)

In February 1784, the return of Banastre Tarleton to his native Liverpool, in order to visit his mother, produced a celebration of unparalleled dimension. Crowds thronged the streets as the entire population turned out to witness the homecoming of their most famous son. In 1792, due to his popularity, Banastre Tarleton was elected as a Member of Parliament for Liverpool and held the position until 1812. It is during this period that he is credited with introducing cricket to his home town. He later married Susan Bertie and retired to private life. He died, without issue, in 1833 and is buried in the Herefordshire village of Leintwardine.

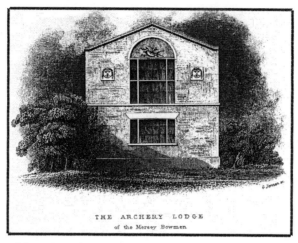

THE ARCHERY LODGE
of the Mersey Bowmen

Consulting the records held by Liverpool Cricket Club, we are told that the game was first played in Liverpool around 1800. The pitch used is thought to be at the home of the Mersey Bowman Archery Club, formed in 1781, at Cazneau Street. Evidence of the clubs existence is confirmed by an article that appeared in a Liverpool newspaper. '*On Thursday last, the Mersey Bowmen held their annual meeting, when a silver medal was shot for, at one hundred yards, and won by William Nicholson, Esq., of Brazenose College, Oxford.*' (Gores General Advertiser, 16th July 1795.)

For their personal comfort the club members built a two storey building. It was at this location that the local sportsmen would congregate making it the most likely spot for the advent of cricket on Merseyside. In 1798 the club left the site and the lodge was taken over by a local Cooper with the name of James MacDonald. The Mersey Bowmen, it is recorded, next moved to Lodge Lane before settling on their present home in Sefton Park. Today the club members concern themselves with the skills of lawn tennis but do, occasionally, still practice the art of toxophily.

The cricket players of Liverpool, in the meantime, had settled into a new home, known as Mosslake Field, at the top of Mount Pleasant. This long eradicated area once formed a plateau that, due to poor drainage, was liable to flood in the winter. The landscape, with the advent of Spring, would dry out allowing the pasture to become covered with the yellow flowers of the plant Bog Myrtle, following which the Liverpool cricket players could be seen on the meadow.

The players would take to the field dressed in the uniform of the day. This consisted of white flannel trousers, linen shirts and a tall black hat known as a 'Billycock'. The playing strip, unlike the manicured surfaces of today, would have been of an uneven nature while the length of the grass would have been determined by the cut of a scythe. (The lawnmower not invented until the 1830s). The game was, at this time, played in accordance with rules that had been laid down in 1808 by The St. Mary-le-Bone Club (MCC). These early exponents of the gentle art quickly established a code of conduct to regulate the future activities of the membership. This set of rules, issued in 1807, is displayed today on the wall of the committee room at Aigburth. The proclamation was worded as follows:

THE ORIGINAL AND UNRIVALLED
MOSSLAKE FIELD CRICKET SOCIETY

1807

We, the undersigned, having become members of the above Society, do hereby agree to stand to and observe the following Laws, Rules and Regulations

FIRST. That every member on admission to this society, by

signing these rules, shall pay to the Treasurer the sum of seven shillings to be considered a part of the General Fund.

SECOND. That everyone of the undersigned members assembled on the field appropriated to their use in Mosslake Fields, on the mornings of Monday, Wednesday and Friday, in each week during the present season or so long as a majority for the time being may think proper to keep the said Society on foot.

THIRD. That 6 o'clock be, and is hereby fixed the hour of attendance on every fixed morning and every member who shall be absent from the field at quarter past six o'clock shall be fined the sum of six pence. If half past six one shilling, If seven o'clock one shilling and six pence and in the case of non-attendance (except as after mentioned) the sum of two shilling.

FOURTH. That all fines shall be received by the Treasurer who shall appropriate the same to the use of the Society and be considered as part of the General Fund.

FIFTH. That there is a President elected every month who shall have the privilege of choosing a Treasurer.

SIXTH. That every dispute which might arise in this Society whether within the field or without shall be decided by a majority of members present in which the President has two votes.

SEVENTH. That no excuse be admitted for non-attendance in any respect unless occasioned by business or sickness in which case notice shall be given to the President or some member who shall next meeting report the same.

EIGHTH. That all fines unpaid within three days after they

shall be incurred shall be doubled, if six days trebled and if unpaid at the end of nine days members so minus shall be dismissed by the Society.

NINTH. That any member shall be at liberty to resign but after his resignation he shall not be admitted again without first paying his entrance money of seven shilling.

An account of the years that followed are faithfully recorded in an article that appeared in a former newspaper named the Liverpool Courier. It was published around the time of the opening, in 1881, of the new ground at Aigburth and appeared under the heading. ... "CRICKET PAST AND PRESENT: THE LIVERPOOL CLUB. *The cricket club was established about the beginning of the century, but of its absolute founders, little is known with any degree of certainty. The oldest member now living however, gives the names of the following gentlemen as among others who, when he joined (1810), took a prominent part and for some years subsequently :-- P & T Leicester, R & J Grayson, R & E Dawson, J Hornby, J Langton, E Stens, G Barnwell, A Smith, E Falkner, R Dirom, P & W Rigby, G Lawrence, J & J Ewart, D & J Willis, W & H Earle, J French, J & S Leigh, S & R Richmond, R Gladstone, E Jones, W Clay, H Birch, W & R Neilson, G Littledale, J Greenwood, Dr Brandreth, C & W Duncan, F Heywood, J & E Peel, H Greenwood. In 1810 the site of the playing pitch was reported to be located to the North-east of Mosslake-Fields on which site Brownlow Hill Workhouse now stands.* (Today the site of the Metropolitan Cathedral of Christ the King). *The club subsequently moved to the South side of Crabtree Lane and about the year 1820, again changed its quarters to a field now covered by Abercromby Square; whilst about ten years later the energies of the times necessitated a further change, and a domicile for many years was found adjacent to the Wavertree Road.*

The local newspapers, who at first paid cricket no attention, eventually published this account of a game that was played in 1817. It is evident by reading this report, that other Liverpool based cricket clubs existed at the time, but no reports of their matches seem to appear in the local press. ... *Cricket - the long expected cricket match between the Liverpool and Edge Hill clubs, was decided yesterday in favour of the latter. The match was won easily, the Edge Hill having nine wickets standing. The contest was extremely interesting, two to one being the general odds at the commencement, and four to one after the first innings in favour of Liverpool. The weather was very favourable, and the attendance numerous.* (Liverpool Mercury, 4th July 1817.)

The first pitch was located in the bottom left hand corner of the picture on the site then occupied by the Workhouse. The second ground was

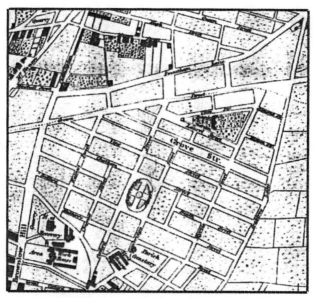

The Mosslake Field area of Liverpool circa 1830

located in the bottom right corner on the south side of Crabtree Lane while the third pitch is now, centre page, covered by Abercomby Square.

The Liverpool Mercury, strange as it may seem, was not the first to report a game involving cricket players from Liverpool. This distinction fell to a newspaper from Yorkshire. The Leeds Intelligencer, (31st August 1812,) made reference to a game played on Newton-le-Willows Racecourse between Liverpool and Rochdale. The contest, which consisted of 2 innings, resulted in a 42 run victory for the players from Rochdale.

The Liverpool Cricket Club was soon to be challenged by other clubs that sprung up from within the town. Evidence of this is provided by a club minute book, now in a private collection, dated from 1822. The book gives dates of fixtures played against such clubs as Brunswick and Chester at a time when runs were recorded by notches on a stick. Noted amongst the members are the names of Earle and Langton. These two families were identified with the commercial and social life of Liverpool and took a prominent share in various departments of public work. They were listed amongst the membership when the club re-issued its rules.

LIVERPOOL CRICKET CLUB, 1ST MAY 1822
Rules

1st That the club shall not exceed 50 members and that all new members shall be chosen by the committee.

2nd That the cricketers shall meet every Wednesday at ten past two o clock.

3rd That fines of 1/- shall be paid by every member not on the field at the appropriate time unless written notice of his inability had been sent to the ground: member out of town or confined to the house by indisposition.

4th That the sides be chosen immediately after the role has been called.

5th That any member leaving the field before the game he has contested in is decided, he shall be fined 1/- : getting a substitute will not excuse the fine.

6th That the home players shall be on the ground.

7th That the marquee shall be erected every Wednesday

8th That all games shall be played according to the Laws of Lords Cricket Ground.

9th That each member subscribe £1-0-0d.

10th That all fines shall be paid on the day on which they are imposed.

11th That no fine shall be paid on days unfit for playing.

12th That Messrs: Birth, Chetwode, French, Leicester, Neilson and Ogilvy shall be the Committee to collect subscriptions, fines and manage the affairs of the club.

N. B. All subjects of detail to be decided by the Committee.

The limited membership was designed to keep the club firmly under the control of the Merchants and Ship Owners of Liverpool and their powerful presence would dictate club policy for many years to come. These men were to forge a strong trading link with the manufacturing town of Manchester. When the Manchester Cricket Club was formed, Liverpool quickly laid down a challenge and in 1823 the sides met for the first time. There is, alas, no account of the game to be found.

An illustration of Liverpool in the 1840s

As this arrangement was made before the dawn of railway travel the Liverpool players had to make the journey to Manchester by horse drawn carriage. This process was relatively straightforward thanks to the benefit of an excellent turnpike route between the two towns. In 1824 the journey, in 3 stages, could be completed in around 3 hours. The most popular point of departure from Liverpool was the Talbot Inn in Water Street. The Stagecoach would then travel to Prescot, where a fresh team of horses would take it on to the Red Lion at Warrington. Once there the passengers would alight for refreshments while the coach company would, for a second time, harness a fresh team of horses. The travellers would then be transported to Irlam from where, after a third change of horses, the carriage would complete its journey to Manchester. In 1830 the world's first major steam railway was opened between Liverpool and Manchester. The Stagecoach companies, who could not survive in the face of such opposition, quickly faded into history.

In 1824 the sides met again at Salford Crescent, Manchester. The match began at 11am and finished just before 8pm in the evening with the home side being victorious by 39 runs. The Liverpool team was as follows: Jas Cooke, W Cooke, R Neilson, H Earle, H Garnett, French, Hurry, Carter, Sneyd, Lloyd-Jones, and Rigby.

The return game, which took place at Crabtree Lane, was won by Liverpool. The visitors, after being bowled out in their first innings, trailed the home side by 10 runs. Liverpool then hit 105 runs in their second innings leaving Manchester to score 127 runs for victory. The total however, was beyond the reach of the Mancunians, who managed only 27 runs, thus leaving Liverpool the winners by 100 runs.

By 1828 the Mosslake Field had been sold and a grid pattern was laid out for houses. The development slowly encroached on the cricket field until, in 1829, Liverpool Cricket Club abandoned their home and moved further out of town. They took over a piece of land on Wavertree Road at the junction of what later became Tunnel Road. The choice of ground is somewhat puzzling as the tranquillity of the surrounding area was already under threat from the construction of the world's first major railway line. Opened on September 15th 1830 it was designed for the transportation of goods between the port of Liverpool and the manufacturing centre of Manchester. The line terminated at Edge Hill where a large Moorish style arch, complete with battlements, was constructed near the edge of the Liverpool Cricket Ground. The future expansion of this railway system would, for many years to come, shape the destiny of Liverpool Cricket Club but they were, for the time being, secure in their new home.

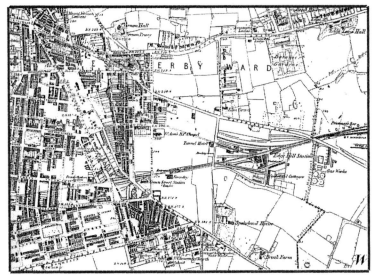

A map of the Edge Hill area of Liverpool printed in 1845

The 1845 map of the area, as illustrated, makes no reference to a permanent site of a cricket ground, while the Tunnel Hotel is the only hostelry anywhere near to where the ground, on Tunnel Road, was reported to be located. It is likely, should this be the case, that a dressing tent would have been pitched on the cricket field to provide shelter from any inclement weather that may have occurred in course of the match as well as a place to eat.

The Junction of Wavertree Road with Tunnel Road

The oil painting (on previous page) from the Beattie collection is housed in the Liverpool Record Office and it depicts a cricket match in progress. The buildings surrounding the field appear to be well advanced in years yet are not shown on the map of 1845. So whether the scene is authentic is open to conjecture. The large chimney stack once belonged to Milners Safe Works. The site was bought by the London and North-Western Railway.

London and North-Western Railway Company had, in 1846 absorbed the Liverpool and Manchester Railway, (now renamed the Grand Junction Railway) into its extensive network, thus giving Liverpool a direct rail link with the Capital. The early passengers, requiring transportation to London would leave from Lime Street and travel to Earlestown where they would join the main line running south in the direction of Warrington and onwards to London. In 1869, to reduce the travelling time, a railway bridge was built to cross the River Mersey between Widnes and Runcorn. This facility enabled the Liverpool train to join the west coast main line south of Warrington at Norton Junction thus enabling the company to transport perishable goods in and out of Liverpool. The site of the former cricket ground was, after purchase, turned into a fruit and vegetable depot.

Liverpool Cricket Club played their last match at Tunnel Road on the 6th of September 1845 and promptly began their search for a new home. They were aided in their quest by a director of the very company to whom they had lost their former home. Sir Hardman Earle, who lived nearby, was the owner of a fine mansion, Spekeland House, and a large estate named Spekefield. The property, eighty eight acres in all, had been bought by his father, Thomas Earle in 1810. When he died in1822, the estate was entrusted into the care of Sir Hardman. The boundaries of the property ran eastwards from Tunnel Road, down along

Smithdown Lane (Road) to Toxteth Brook and then northwards as far as Wavertree Road, from where it turned westwards back to Tunnel Road. Sir Hardman, along with his brother William, had, from the outset, been connected with the cricket playing fraternity of Liverpool. He was now a director of L & N W Railway and offered to lease the cricket club a small section of the Spekefield estate. The pasture was situated between Sandy Lane and a small cluster of well maintained cottages occupied by workers employed on the railway.

The area surrounding the new ground was, to a certain degree, already beginning to show signs of urban advancement. The railway line to London ran the length of one side of the field while the storage tanks belonging to the new Liverpool Gas Company presented an imposing presence on the other side of Sandy Lane. The Liverpool cricket players paying these portents no attention pushed on and planned for the future.

In 1847 they took possession of the Spekefield ground and quickly laid it out for cricket. The early matches, apart from the visit of the Manchester Club, were played amongst the members and players, who they considered to be of equal social standing. Towards the end of the season the ground was honoured with its first important game. The fourteen of Liverpool, which included W. Lilywhite and W. Martingell, took on the XI of England. The match, which ran out of daylight, ended in a draw.

Liverpool Cricket Club soon settled in at their new home and quickly built an impressive pavilion to shelter the members from the elements. The single storey structure made entirely of timber, contained dressing rooms and a refectory that could also be used for social functions. The building was fronted by a long open porch that was supported by strong wooden posts. The limits of the playing field were eventually enclosed by a high stone wall in the years that followed. This enabled the club, if they so desired, to make a charge at the gate. The care of the pavilion was, in later years, placed in the hands of a married couple, who, with their well stocked kitchen and elaborate food tables, earned the praise of an unknown author who penned the following article:-

... *"In those days the ground was reached either by omnibus, cab or railway to Edge Hill Station, then after jumping over innumerable railway lines, carrying a heavy carpet bag and hurling over the wall which had to be climbed, the enthusiastic cricketers arrived at a low rambling structure which served as a pavilion. This was in charge of a man and his wife, who on match days provided a meal consisting of ponderous joints, beefsteaks, fruit tarts and massive cheeses. One hour was allowed for this meal, but with luck the game was restarted no later than 3.15, by which time the younger members of the team had returned from a hasty visit to their respective offices, where after having exhibited an invoice or account sales to their seniors, as they had been working, they jumped into a fly or cab and returned to the ground. On rare occasions a dinner was given to the visitors and the evening usually closed with singing or even dancing".*

The married couple referred to in this article is almost certainly Mr. & Mrs May who took charge of the catering in other major cricket matches that were staged in Liverpool. The items they displayed on the menu seemed to increase along with the wealth of the brokers and merchants of Liverpool. The Port of Liverpool, thanks to its seaborne trade with the Americas was, by 1850, the largest importer of cotton in the United Kingdom. As much as 80% of this raw commodity was shipped in before being moved by rail to east Lancashire to be processed. Once this had been done the goods were then transported back to the bustling seaport where they were reloaded and shipped out for export. The proceeds of this highly lucrative process were to generate a great amount of wealth for the merchants, brokers and ship-owners of Liverpool. Many of these gentlemen, looking to improve the quality of their leisure time, continued to form a strong bond with the cricket club at Spekefields.

Liverpool Cricket Club, thanks to the benevolent patronage of these individuals, soon became the wealthiest group of sportsmen based in the Merseyside area. The fixture secretary was now able to look further afield and arrange regular meetings with the military personnel who were stationed both locally and at Preston. On 28th August 1852, the Liverpool Club took the ferry to Dublin where they played a game against the Phoenix Park Club. This jaunt became an annual event that soon included matches played at Phoenix Park against the army regiments, who were, at the time, stationed at Dublin Castle. The Liverpool XI would, on the odd occasion, turn the rudder in the direction of Belfast and help the development of the game in Ulster. Here they would meet a representative XI, who played as the North of Ireland, on the Ballynafiegh Cricket Ground in Belfast.

It was around this time that the Liverpool ground, due to its many improvements, was acknowledged in the Lilywhites Cricket Guide of England. The reporter, who visited around 1850, appears to have left the train at Edge Hill thinking it was the end of the line. … *"The Liverpool Cricket Club ground is situated close to the terminus and is enclosed within a stone wall and hedge. Its size is from 15 to 20 acres. An excellent pavilion is erected on the North side of the ground where every accommodation can be afforded. The club consists of some very fine players."*

The Liverpool Club, thanks to the improvements made to rail travel, could now begin to arrange fixtures with leading clubs from other parts of Lancashire. The Western Club, from Eccles, began to put in an annual appearance along with the Castleton Club from Rochdale. The Club was now in a position to engage the regular services of a professional bowler whose name was William Parry. He was a native of Oxfordshire and he made his debut against the Cestrian Club in 1854. Mr. Perry was employed to bowl at the members and to take charge of the maintenance of the playing field. His presence at Spekefields was to further enhance the quality of batting displayed by the Liverpool members. He served the club for fifteen years before he was, on his retirement, replaced by the son of Mrs May. The Spekefield club, despite these many improvements, now suddenly faced competition from a new development that was about to take place in Liverpool.

Richard Vaughan Yeats, a local entrepreneur, submitted plans to build an area of high quality housing on the southern outskirts of the town. The neighbourhood, part of Toxteth Park, was to be set around the sides of a small wooded valley where Mr. Yeats, by his own enterprise, intended to create an area of public parkland. The man he employed to carry out this task, Joseph Paxton, began work in 1840. He swiftly surrounded the area with a road which he named after his main patron, The Duke of Devonshire. He then dammed the rivulet that ran through the bottom of the dell in order to establish a lake. The stream, known locally as "Dickenson's Dingle", was named after the local fisherman who lived near its confluence with the River Mersey. Mr Paxton next surrounded the lake with winding footpaths that were lined with flowerbeds and ornate shelters. A large palatial mansion was sited at the head of the lake giving the prospect an almost regal appearance. The area immediately surrounding the lake was shaped with moderate contours while what remained of the available land was levelled out for recreation.

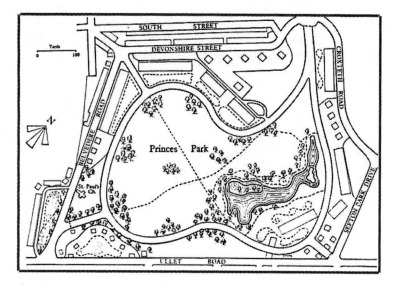

Princes Park Liverpool

Mr Yeats, in the meantime, began to build a ring of large houses that faced in on to the parkland. He then laid out a large wide boulevard that approached the park from the direction of Liverpool town centre. At the head of the boulevard he placed a westward facing set of wrought iron gates that were designed to catch the rays of the afternoon sun. In 1845 the setting was given the name of Princes Park in deference to Prince Albert. The death of Mr Yeats, on 30th November 1856, produced a profound feeling of grief amongst the local population and many of them attended his internment at the ancient chapel on Park Road. A memorial was later erected in his honour at the main entrance to Princes Park.

The area was soon inhabited by many of Liverpool's wealthy families who flocked to the park in their recreation hours. The clean surroundings were, for many, a welcome relief from the smoke filled atmosphere of the town centre. Each Sunday, when the weather permitted, large crowds could be seen promenading along the banks of the lake. The younger men of the area, in pursuit of a healthy lifestyle, found that the flat areas of the park were an ideal place in which to indulge themselves in their love of cricket. They quickly formed a resident team which they named Liverpool Olympus.

On August 7th 1848, the Liverpool Club made their first appearance at Princes Park to take on the latest introduction to the local cricket scene. The game, played over two days, was won by Liverpool by 97 runs. It was played on the western side of the location near to its Devonshire Road boundary and it was here that other important matches were to take place. A professional England Eleven visited Princes Park on five occasions from 1852 onwards, the last of these games, June 15th 1857, was witnessed by a Liverpool journalist who described the scene in the manner of the day. ...

The match of 1857 will long be remembered with feeling of pleasure by all who had the opportunity of witnessing it. The weather was everything that could be desired - fair, clear, and just enough wind to keep the heat from being oppressive. The ground in the Princes Park, as on former occasions, was enclosed with canvas and within the enclosure a large marquee was erected for the purpose of refreshment. Here Mrs May, of Wavertree presided, the mention of whose name is sufficient to characterize the quality of the provision and the manner in which it was dispensed. The tent, and that belonging to Princes Park Club, was very gaily decorated with flags. There were seats provided for visitors extending around the whole of the ground. A printing press was in operation to supply returns on the fall of each wicket. And the band of the Royal Pensioners was in attendance. Harmonious strains from which assisted most materially to give effect to the scene. The attendance of youth and beauty, combined with feminine grace and excellent taste in dress and dignity of carriage added much to the brilliance of the assembly.

(Liverpool Albion 22nd June 1857.)

The match was played under the title of the XI of England v 22 of Liverpool. The professional players showed no uniformity in their dress yet were extremely careful in the manner in which they played the game. The local amateurs, in marked contrast, appeared over dressed for the occasion and one or two of them wore pink and scarlet shirts. The 22 of Liverpool, after taking a first innings lead, lost the match by 47 runs.

Over at Wavertree the Liverpool committee took note of the challenge that was now posed by Princes Park and arranged a quality match on their own ground. On 28th August 1857 a 'United All England XI' faced the 22 of the Liverpool Club. John Wisden and John Lillywhite were included in the visiting team while Liverpool employed the services of four professional bowlers. The weather was all that could be desired and there was a large crowd of spectators surrounding the field of play.

The home side, which batted first, was bowled out for a total of 89 runs. The visitors were then dismissed by the professional bowling of Brompton and Hinkly. They were all out for 78 runs. Brompton (Notts) then hit 40 of the 120 runs made by the Liverpool side in their second innings, leaving the visitors to score 132 runs to win. The bowling of Brompton and Hinkly once again proved too powerful for the England XI who, in their second innings, were dismissed for a total of 63 runs, Liverpool thus winning the match quite comfortably.

Princes Park, unlike its future neighbour Sefton Park, was never to feature a designated cricket ground within its boundaries.

This was perhaps due to the fact that the location was a private development and, until 1918, did not belong to the Liverpool Parks and Gardens. The Olympus team was soon superseded by Dingle Cricket Club who remained at the location until around the turn of the century. Today no cricket clubs play their home matches on Princes Park.

The Liverpool Club, despite the threat from Princes Park, continued their ascendancy amongst the local cricket clubs. Their status as the leading club was confirmed when, on 19th July 1859, the Wavertree location received the first visit of the famous Zingari Cricket Club. The Zingari (the Italian word for Gypsy) was a nomadic organization that was made up of well appointed gentlemen. They came mainly from the South of England and were drawn from the elite of Victorian society. Their visit greatly enhanced the prestige of the Liverpool ground which, later that year, was to host a first class cricket fixture.

11th August 1859 The Gentlemen of the South v The Gentlemen of the North

The Southern side was made up of county players, four of them from the Walker family of Surrey. The rest of the side was made up of players from either Surrey of Sussex. The Northern side consisted mainly of varsity players with no county experience. They were led by Joe Makinson of Cambridge University while William Horner was the only Liverpool born man in the line up. The South, as expected, won the game by 85 runs.

On 16th July 1861 the Zingari C.C. took part in a two day match at Spekefields which they won by 33 runs. A sports reporter, commissioned by the Liverpool Daily Post to cover the game, made the following remarks. ... *The match, which occupied the two last days, has been productive of some first rate sport, both parties playing with great spirit. The attendance on both days, especially of the fair sex, was very large; and, although the Liverpool Gentlemen were doomed to defeat, they have the satisfaction of knowing that their opponents consisted of the finest amateurs in England.* Fair comment and good observation it may well have been, but the report failed to find favour with the editor of a certain Liverpool based magazine of the day. It was published under the name of Porcupine.

Porcupine was a weekly magazine that was designed to pass comment on the everyday affairs in the lives of the people of Liverpool. It began publication in 1821 and ceased in 1881. It claimed to be a journal of current events - Social, Political and Satirical The magazine printed an article criticizing the selection of certain Liverpool players who, it claimed, were included in the team merely to increase their social standing. It did, however, stop short of mentioning anybody by name.

"The Liverpool Club does a Snobbish Thing."

Everyone who takes an interest in the manly and national game of cricket knows that the Liverpool Cricket Club suffered a most inglorious defeat lately at the hands of the Zingari Club. Porcupine knows the reason why, Liverpool Cricket Club sacrificed their reputation to snobbery.

Now if there is one place that ought to be free from the vulgar snobbery of our "parrenu" swells, it is the cricket field. Here all classes ought to meet on equal terms, and merit alone ought to determine the standard of a man engaged in our peculiar national game. According to the Saturday Review (a rival publication) this is not the case, but the worthy Editor of our contemporary never played cricket at Liverpool, or he would have discovered that the "modern tyre", the wretched spirit of caste, intrudes in to our most hearty and universal amusement. But the fact is the Zingari club is composed of gentlemen of considerable society position and when they visit Liverpool, Lord Sefton hospitably entertains them at Croxteth, inviting their opponents also to his little Hall. Now, of course, for the honour of dining with a Lord, the most magnificent, self satisfied and insolent "swell" that ever sold a bale of cotton, a hogshead of tallow, or a puncheon of rum, will make any sacrifice, even of own self respect, or his pride in the glories of his cricket club.

The opponents of Zingari were therefore carefully selected, not with reference to their skill as cricketers, but with an eye to what is thought of as "Change" of their social status, the result, was natural. (Porcupine 27 July 1861.)

A Cricket Match in Victorian England

27th August 1863 The North v The South

This is the second first class match to have taken place at the home of the Liverpool Club at Spekefields. The game, won by the North, mirrored the changes in the game that were taking place at the time, in the game of cricket in the North of England. The home side included county players from Yorkshire along with professionals from Nottingham. The team from the South was made up of county players and was captained by the experienced Heathfield Stephenson of Surrey. They also included Mr Edward Grace of Bristol.

Moves were now afoot, amongst the principal cricket clubs of Lancashire, to form a team that was to truly represent the county. The objective was to emulate the county sides that were already regularly competing in first class cricket fixtures, most noticeable in the South. The initial meeting took place on 12th January 1864, at the Queens Hotel in Manchester. The host town was represented by the clubs of Manchester, Broughton, Longsight, and Western while Liverpool, Huyton and Northern attended on behalf of the Merseyside area. Blackburn and Accrington spoke for East Lancashire while Wigan Oldham and Ashton represented the clubs from their respective district. It was agreed, after a lengthy discussion, that a county side should be formed and that the side would be based on not one ground, but play at all the major venues in Lancashire. When this was decided upon, all the parties made their way home to await their allocation of the fixtures.

23rd August 1866 Lancashire v Surrey

This was the first game of county cricket to take place in Liverpool. The occasion was well received by the local cricket followers who, in great numbers, assembled to welcome the popular Surrey team to the Spekefield ground. The two sides, following a brief exchange of courtesies, began their match at 12: 30. The southerners, who won the toss, took to the field followed by Lancashire openers Gideon Holgate and Thomas Owen Potter.

Lancashire soon lost vital wickets against the experienced bowling of Griffith, Humphrey and Jupp. T. O. Potter, batting on his home wicket, offered stubborn resistance before being dismissed on 39. Nevertheless a ninth wicket stand, by F Reynolds and A Appleby added 42 runs as the home side were dismissed for a total of 125 runs. The crowd that had built up steadily now framed the pitch in great numbers as Surrey began their reply. The Lancashire bowlers now showed their mettle leaving the visitors 87 for 6 at the close of play.

Another large attendance, in anticipation of Lancashire victory, thronged the Spekefields ground as play began on the second day. The visitors, restored by a good nights rest, hit back during the morning session to end their innings on 119. The Surrey bowling partnership of Humphrey and Griffith then proved too much for the home side that collapsed to a second innings total of 86 runs. The visitors, needing 93 to win, displayed an element of uncertainty as they struggled to 73 for 7. Nevertheless an eighth wicket stand by Pooley and Griffith guided Surrey home to victory by 3 wickets. The Londoners spent the night in Liverpool and returned home the next morning. The first Lancashire match, despite the defeat, had been well attended and enjoyed by the indigenous population. Sadly they had to wait another 15 years until the county side was to be seen again in Liverpool.

Thomas Owen "Thosper" Potter

This was the only time that T O Potter was selected to play for Lancashire. Born in 1814 'Thosper' (his popular nickname) was born into a wealthy family of cotton merchants in Calcutta. They later moved to Liverpool where 'Thosper', along with his brother William, frequently opened the batting on the old Liverpool ground at Wavertree. He later moved to the Wirral and played cricket for Birkenhead Park. William continued to play his cricket with Liverpool and on 11th August 1870 he played for Lancashire against Surrey at the Oval. 'Thosper' meanwhile, helped to establish the first golf club in the north of England at Hoylake. He devoted much of his time to this new venture and soon became a prominent member. The club is to-day, thanks to the patronage of The Duke of Connaught, known as the Royal Liverpool Golf Club. T. O. Potter died at Hoylake in 1909.

29th April 1872 North of England v South of England

This match was the last first class game to be played on the Spekefield ground at Wavertree. It did, by team selection, go some way to illustrate the further changes that had recently taken place within the game of cricket in the North of England. Seven of the home side now played county cricket with Yorkshire. The Southern team contained four players from Sussex and five from Surrey while two players from Gloucestershire made up the numbers. The immortal W G Grace, along with his brother Fred, made his only appearance on the Spekefield ground. The visitors proved too strong for the Northerners, who lost the match by an innings and 20 runs.

1.C.Todd	10.D.Cunningham	19.Alfred Fletcher
2.H.H.Hornb	11.D.C.Fraser	20.W.Horner
3.Tranter	12.Wm. Langton	21.T.O.Potter
4.W.May	13.W.Todd	22.Arthur P.Fletcher
5.A.Eccles	14.G.Bromfield	23.
6.H.F.Hornby	15.Geo.Blythe	24.Arthur Earle
7.T.D.Hornby	16.T.R.Stolterfoht	25.D.Carstairs
8.Chas Langton	17.E.J.Thornewill	26.E.W.Rayner
9.F.Napier	18.	27.W.T.Pears

A picture of the club members taken at Spekefields

It was around this time that a representative XI of the Liverpool Club began a series of annual matches that became known as the "School Tours". A heavy leather-bound book, recording the earliest of these matches, may still be found to-day in the pavilion at Aigburth. The book details the matches which took place each year during the Whitsuntide Holiday. They were played against some of the leading public schools of England including: Marlborough, Cheltenham, Eton and Clifton. The book also contains several photographs of the players who competed in the opening games.

The Liverpool Team (year unknown)
at Cheltenham College

The tours were to prove a great success and provided Liverpool Cricket Club with a good supply of up and coming young players. It is also worth mentioning that, during a match against Clifton School in 1891, a young man came in to bat at number 11. His name was W G Grace junior. The tours ended during the 1930s due to the change in the social climate.

No historical account of Liverpool Cricket would be complete without mentioning the outstanding contribution made by the Steel brothers. Several members of the family played for Liverpool and four were selected for Lancashire.

Douglas Quintin Steel. Born in Liverpool on 19 June 1856 he attended Uppingham College and Cambridge University where he soon developed into an all round cricketer. In 1876 he gained his 'Blue' and played the first of his 22 matches for Lancashire He was also a great football player and represented Cambridge at both rugby and soccer. On 9 July 1884 he set a Merseyside record by scoring 226 runs in a club match against local rivals, Sefton. The visitors, who occupied the crease all day, scored 478 runs. He died at Upton-by Chester on 2 December 1933.

Allen Gibson Steel. Without doubt the most famous cricketer to have played for the Liverpool Club. Known by the moniker of "NAB" he was born on 24 September 1858 in West Derby. He attended Marlborough College and was selected to play in the school side against Rugby School at Lords, at the age of 15. He was a right handed batsman and a fine medium pace bowler. Allen Steel made his first class debut at the age of 19 for Lancashire against Sussex before he went "up" to Cambridge in 1878. He was in the great Cambridge elevens between 1878 and 1881 and captained the side for two seasons.

In 1882 he was picked to play for England in the initial test match against Australia at the Oval. He went on to play 13 times for his country and captained them on three occasions. In 1883 he played his finest innings at Sydney where, against the bowling of Spofforth and Boyle, he scored 135 runs without the loss of his wicket. In 1894 he made his last first class appearance at Aigburth. He was part of the Liverpool & District XI who lost to a Cambridge University side that included a young Ranjitsinhji. He played in all 162 games of first class cricket, scoring 7,000 runs and taking 789 wickets. He later left Liverpool to work as a Barrister in London and, in 1902, became President of the MCC. He died in London on 15 June 1916.

Harold Banner Steel. Born in Liverpool 9 April 1862, he attended Repton before going up to Cambridge where he was injured at football and played no cricket. He recovered from this setback and, after making his debut in 1883, played 22 times for

Lancashire. He could have played more games for his county but preferred to play his cricket for Liverpool. In 1884, during the match against Sefton, he joined his brother at the crease and hit a lightening century. He died in Burnham, Somerset on 29 June 1911.

Ernest Eden Steel. Born in Liverpool on 25 June 1864, he attended Marlborough College and played against the Liverpool touring side in 1880. No record exists of his cricket while at University but, after making his debut in 1884, he played 40 times for Lancashire. He died on 25 June 1924 in Southport.

As the years rolled by the club members, would, for their own amusement, divide themselves in to sides with an eccentric collection of names. These included line ups selected by such divisions as: age, height, former school and letters of the alphabet. These extra games made for a full season and ensured that most of the members, who so desired, could enjoy the occasional game of cricket. Not even the great W G Grace, who was appearing on the ground of Sefton, could prevent the pre-arranged match played between the first XI and 18 veterans, from going ahead at the Wavertree ground.

Liverpool Cricket Club continued to play at Wavertree until, in 1877, the land was sold for development. The railway company, in order to lay extra track, took possession of the cricket field. They skirted the edge of the ground with sidings that were designed to serve an iron foundry that was planned for the future. The final game, against Phoenix Park, ended in a victory by 6 wickets and, on Saturday 8 September 1877, the stumps at the old Spekefield ground were drawn for the last time. Liverpool Cricket Club now spent three years in the wilderness as the old ground disappeared under the wheels of progress.

Liverpool Cricket Club, following their departure from the

Wavertree area, was praised in the local press for the consideration shown to their former employees. The Liverpool Courier had this to say on the occasion. … *"Unlike many other clubs, Liverpool has not been unmindful of the old and faithful servants and changes were seldom made. Perry, a fine bowler, rendered service to the club for a period of about 15 years and May, his successor, for seven; while "Old Joe" (Joseph Hooley), as ground repairer and general assistant, was in the service of the club for over 30 years, during seven of which, when old and infirm, he received a pension, which was continued to the day of his death. Watt Hughes, from a boy, rose to the position of under groundsman, and after fourteen years service, left on the break-up of the Edge Hill ground. Of others, it may be mentioned that Mrs Davis, who lived on the ground, was perhaps one of the oldest servants of the club, her labours extending over a period of thirty five years."* Part of the old ground was soon covered with terraced housing and the streets named after famous Australian cricketers such as Field and Murdoch. Sandy Lane was the last to go as its title, in deference to the "Demon Bowler", was changed to Spofforth Road. The Iron Works, which had only a short life, was soon closed down and the area was covered with more houses. Liverpool Cricket Club meanwhile, was without a home.

Sir William Philip Molyneux, the 4th Earl of Sefton, heard of the club's plight and quickly came to its aid. The noble Lord, in a most kindly gesture, offered the club the use of his own private cricket ground on his estate at West Derby. The well maintained pitch, which had its own pavilion, was laid out in beautiful parkland directly in front of Croxteth Hall. There was no finer environment in England in which to play cricket.

The club, with its players safe for a while at Croxteth, now set out in search of a new home which they hoped would be theirs in perpetuity. Soliciting the help of the wealthiest men in Liverpool, they formed a new business enterprise with the intention of building the finest cricket ground yet seen in England. It was decided after several meetings, to adopt the title of the "Liverpool and South West Lancashire Cricket Ground Company 1880". The new corporation quickly purchased ten acres of arable land on the outskirts of Liverpool at Aigburth. The area already displayed signs of affluence and could be reached by train, alighting at Mersey Road railway station. This amenity was operated by the Cheshire Lines Committee. The name of this Company was perhaps a little misleading as the vast majority of its railway lines lay within the county of Lancashire. The service offered by the committee was noted for its punctuality and they operated the swiftest link, (around 40 minutes) between Liverpool and Manchester. The Cheshire Lines Committee was, in 1932, responsible for the transportation of over 1/5 of goods that were unloaded from the docks at Liverpool. Such a rail link was vital if the Liverpool Club hoped to entice cricket fans from outside the immediate area.

Work on the new pavilion was started without delay. The structure, designed by Mr. Harrison, was to be built on three levels. The ground floor, set aside as a service area, contained the kitchen and washing rooms for the players. The second tier contained two large rooms plus a bar area, while the top floor, served by a wide staircase, contained a spacious changing room that was fronted by a south facing balcony. The contract for this prodigious venture was awarded to the building firm of Cubbits, while the task of producing a horizontal playing pitch was placed in the hands of a Mr Thomas of St Anne's on Sea. This gentleman supervised the draining and levelling of the field before it was overlaid with salt washed Cumberland turf. The total cost of the pitch project was estimated to be £260.

Mr Thomas was to later lay the pitch at Old Trafford.

The players meanwhile, began their exploits at Croxteth with a game against Kersal. The appointed players next made their annual public school tour before returning home to assist in a variety of fixtures against teams from the Liverpool area. The visit of the Zingari XI, returning after a long absence, proved to be the highlight of the season but the match with the Australian touring side was lost to Stanley Cricket Club. The season at Croxteth, which proved most enjoyable, ended with a home game against Anfield.

As the new season approached Liverpool Cricket Club managed to arrange a programme of matches that were to be played on the grounds of other local cricket teams. The committee in the meantime, pushed ahead with building work at Aigbuth. This fact was verified by an article that appeared in a local newspaper. ... *"The Liverpool Club offers but a meagre list owing to their ground being in an unfinished state and does not play a match of any importance at home."* (Liverpool Daily Post, 8th of May, 1880.)

The truth of the matter was that Liverpool Cricket Club had to endure two seasons without a home ground to call their own. They continued with the regular tour matches but were forced, in their need for practice, to depend on the kindness of other local cricket clubs. The most benevolent of these was Childwall who allowed their neighbours the regular use of the facilities in place at their ground on Well Lane. So it was, despite the long disruption, that Liverpool Cricket Club ended their long exile with the nucleus of the side still intact. They could now "winter well" and await, with great anticipation, the opening of their new home at Aigburth.

CHAPTER 2

A New Home at Aigburth

The new site at Aigburth had been purchased from two local landowners. A strip of land, to build the pavilion, had been bought from a Mr Daniel Lowe while the large adjacent area was formerly the property of Thomas Baley. Work had continued throughout the winter of 1880/81 and, as Spring approached, the ground was ready to be occupied. The pavilion was far from complete but it was, at this stage, suitable for occupation.

There was some confusion as to how the arrangement with the South-West Lancashire Cricket Company and the prospective rent payers, Liverpool Cricket Club, would operate. Eventually the tenure was decided. The Cricket Club would take out a **twenty five year lease on the ground at a rent of two hundred pounds a year.**

Five years into this agreement the South-West Lancashire Cricket Company discovered that the piece of ground the other side of the railway was up for sale. Fearing that it would be used for housing and thus affect their investment they quickly bought the ground and offered it to the Club. A more robust bridge had to be built to join the two grounds.

The arrangement lasted until 1904 when the Lancashire & South West Cricket Company made an offer to their tenants at Aigburth. They offered to sell their shares (351 in all) at £25 each and clear off their debt of £2,500 at the bank. The only condition was that the 93 shareholders become life members of the Liverpool Club and that the ground, if it were to be sold, could only be used for Cricket. As £23, 000 had been spent since the outset this was a most generous offer. The Liverpool Club, without sufficient funds, decided to issue 351 debentures, at £25 each that paid an interest of £3 per annum on each item.

The transaction was completed on the condition that the club be able to buy back the shares at six months' notice should funds allow. On completion of the sale the Lancashire & South West Cricket Company went into liquidation.

SHAREHOLDERS OF THE LIVERPOOL AND SOUTH WEST

LANCASHIRE CRICKET GROUND COMPANY LTD. 1880

Arkle. J.	Eccles. A.	Melly. G.
Alexander. R.	Eden. J.	Mellor. J.
Adamson. W.	Earle. Sir. T.	Napier. F.
Boult. H.	Edmonson. E.	Newton. T.
Best. T.	Fraser. J.	Parker. A.&S.
Brocklebank. T.	Field. S.	Pilkington. L.
Brocklebank. T. Jnr.	Fletcher. J.	Pilkington. G.
Brocklebank. H.&R.	Gossage. F.	Pilkington. T.
Bowring. W.	Gair. H.	Pilkington. G.
Brancker. C.	Gilmour. H.	Patterson. W.
Brown. A.	Garnett. A.	Pears. W.
Bourne. T.	Gladstone. A.	Parr. H.
Belcher. M.	Gladstone R.	Potter. T. W.
Boddy. G.	Gale. J.	Rathbone. B.&P.
Bibby. J.	Hornby. T. H. C.	Rowe. H.
Bingham. T.	Horsfall. C.&R.	Rayner E.&O.
Bateson. A.	Harvey. E.	Robinson. J.
Bateson. H. D.	Heywood. A.	Rogerson. T.
Bateson. J.	Holt. R. D.	Rowe. C.
Bateson. D. O.	Hay. I.	Radley. J.
Bird. C.	Irvine. T.	Sefton. Earl of
Bates. E.	Johnson. W.	Steel. J.&A.
Barratt. W.	Kelloch. C.	Singlehurst. R.
Birkett. J.	Kewley. J.	Sinclair. S.
Bowes. J.	Lowe. J. C.	Tate. H.
Banner. J.	Laird. M.	Tod. W.
Cunningham. D.	Leyland. R.	Tod. A.
Crosfield. J.&W.	Langton. C.	Timmis. T.
Crookes. R.&J.	Lathom. Earl of	Turner. A.
Cox. G.&J.	Lyster. G.	Tilney. R.
Crosby. C.	Mawdsley. J.	Thompson. G.
Coddington. R.	Maxwell. J.	Wilson. J.
Derby. Earl of	Minoprio. C.	Williams. O.
Duckworth. W.&J.	Maples. A.	Wood. J.
Dobell. G.&A.	McIntyre. L.	Williamson. F.
Davies. J.&E.	Moss. W.	Willis. H.

This list of shareholders reveals the names of many wealthy Liverpool
families along with certain members of the aristocracy

1881

The gates at the new ground were opened for the first time on 30th April 1881. The opposition on this memorable occasion was provided by local neighbours, Dingle. The visitors were a well respected organization who included several public school men amongst their ranks. They were captained by Henry Miller, a fine all round cricketer and a former pupil of Uppingham School. The unsettled weather, however, kept down the crowd who were asked to pay 6 pence at the gate. (Considering the abject poverty less than 5 miles away, this was a considerable amount of money!) The rain did little to deter the more affluent members of the club who were able to watch the game under the cover provided by their private carriages.

The toss was won by Mr Miller who sportingly allowed the resident team to open the batting. The Liverpool innings was opened by G Dunlop, who received the first ball, accompanied by Edward Kewley. Liverpool went on to reach a total of 165 against the excellent bowling of Miller who finished with figures of 7/42. F Williamson, who batted number 10, went in to the record books by hitting the first six on the new ground. The Liverpool bowling was opened by E Steel who, by the dismissal of Lott, became the first home player to take a wicket on the ground. Dingle reached 25 for 2 before the rain increased and forced the play to be abandoned. The first match on the Aigburth ground ended in a draw.

The local press, present in great numbers, covered the event and described the scene thus:- ... *"Saturday was anything but a propitious day for outdoor sports and cricket in particular, a drizzling rain falling until about half past six, at which time it began to come down heavily, so that, notwithstanding the opportunity the match afforded for seeing the new ground of our premier club, it is not to be wondered at that the attendance of the general public was by no means large. There were several carriages present on the ground and many ladies graced the pavilion with their presence, together with a host of the principal patrons of the club. The ground itself, with its belting of trees and shrubs, looked admirable but surroundings of the pavilion - a large handsome and commodious structure - as yet scarcely complete and therefore the erection was not seen to its best advantage. A uniform charge of 6d was made to all parts of the ground - pavilion excepted - and at this figure, given a good match and a fine day no doubt visitors will be numerous. The committee is not unmindful of the public convenience, and is contemplating the building of sheltering houses and a refreshment booth at the railway side - both very necessary things on a cricket field."* (Liverpool Daily Post, 2nd May, 1881.)

13th June - Lancashire v Cambridge University

This match marked the official opening of the Aigburth ground. The Cantabs, aided by A G Steel, opened the batting in front of a crowd of around 2,000 people. (This number, aided by the bright sunshine, had increased to over 5,000 by lunchtime). The flip of a coin, which proved decisive, fell in favour of Cambridge, who elected to bat on a pitch that looked in perfect condition. G Studd, who opened the batting, hit an unbeaten 106, as Cambridge was bowled out for 185. The new wicket however, had cut up badly during the innings and it now favoured the bowling side. Lancashire, who could not overcome these problems, was bowled out for 71 at the end of the first day. The home side, forced to follow on, continued to struggle on the following morning. They were bowled out for a second time leaving the Cantabs to score 38 runs to win. This they did with 7 wickets to spare. The match, scheduled for three days, was over in less than two leaving a small element of the spectators in a rather disgruntled frame of mind. Newspaper journalists from both Liverpool and Manchester were at the game, two of whom made the following comments. ...

"There was one thing struck me as being very pronounced, and that was the prejudice, not to say the animus, displayed by the up-country visitors towards the Liverpool men in the county team, and to account for it is a puzzler. The arrangements of the committee were first class, and the catering for the general public could not have been placed in better hands than those of A C Doe of Roby." (Liverpool Daily Post, 18 June 1881.)

"This, the first match in which the county of Lancashire Eleven have engaged a team on the new ground of the Liverpool Cricket Club at Aigburth, was commenced yesterday, the weather being simply charming and a great contrast to the cold wind and frequent showers sustained the previous week at Old Trafford. The new field of the seaport cricketing organization an admirable one in every respect and beautifully situated amongst surrounding trees and shrubs. A handsome pavilion built from the design of Mr Harrison, architect of Liverpool, ornaments one side of the enclosure, the erection being replete with every convenience, and affording plenty of admirable seating accommodation for the members of the county and local clubs. The arrangements for the match were fairly good, although a certain amount of red tapeism prevailed, which tended to impede the reporters in the discharge of their duties. This is the first season in which the ground has been played upon and the wicket, which was nothing extra to speak about when the play commenced, wore very badly." (Manchester Guardian 14th June 1881.)

The Liverpool Club, in their first year at Aigburth, began to re-establish fixtures with the leading clubs in Lancashire such as Manchester, Preston and Western (Eccles). The stronger Merseyside clubs, such as Northern, and Birkenhead Park, also featured on the fixture list along with sides drawn from the military. The new wicket cut up badly towards the end of the season, due to so many games having been played on it.

It must not be forgotten that cricket was not the only sport that was played at Aigburth. Tennis courts were built at the side of the main pavilion and a thriving tennis section was formed. Ladies were not allowed to join the club but could become lady subscribers with no voting rights or entry into the club house.

Work on the main pavilion continued throughout the closed season and was, as Spring approached, beginning to fill its design. The building, the finest in the country, now put its rival at Old Trafford very much in the shade. The energetic committee soon had the lawns and ornamental gardens which surrounded the Pavilion laid out to perfection and a Ladies Pavilion was built on the eastern side of the ground. The building was a simple construction made mostly of timber but it did have the benefit of two fireplaces made of brick. A female servant was employed to light the fires and see to the needs of the lady members. This was no easy task as the building had neither electricity nor running water so all refreshments had to be carried across from the main building. A neat lawn, surrounded by railings, was later laid in front of the building from which all male members were excluded. The ladies entered this little enclosure by means of a gate that had been conveniently placed in the wall on the Beechwood Road side of the ground.

The Winter break was also used to repair the damage done to the wicket. The committee now engaged the services of George Upsdall the former groundsman at Childwall Cricket Club in the hope of improving the pitch. The venue however, was allocated just one county game, against Nottinghamshire, for the following season.

1882

The visits of Dingle and Childwall got the season off to a quiet start before a large crowd assembled for the visit of Birkenhead Park. On May 22nd in a game against New Brighton, Liverpool reached a total that has yet to be surpassed at the Aigburth ground. The home side occupied the crease for the whole of the day and D Q Steel 111, G Bird 127, and A G Lyster 128 all passed the century mark. Liverpool Cricket Club, when the stumps were drawn, had amassed a total of 500 runs for the loss of 7 wickets. This display of batting cleared up any uncertainty with regards to the playing strip at Aigburth.

Mention must be made here that the only other sport that 'Lady Subscribers' were allowed to play was tennis. This sport is such an important part of the club that a separate history is to be found later in this book.

20th July - Lancashire v Nottinghamshire

The committee erected a large temporary grandstand along the Riversdale Road side of enclosure in anticipation of a large crowd. Added to this was a second stand that ran adjacent to the railway side. The weather however, once again, proved unfavourable. The sky was overcast when Lancashire, who won the toss, opened the batting. The Notts bowlers, who had the better of the first day, dismissed Lancashire for a disappointing score of 93 runs. The visitors watched by a crowd of 4,000 ended the day 100 for 6. Nottingham recommenced their innings and was bowled out for 164 before the play was interrupted by rain. Lancashire, who batted between the showers, ended the second day on 56 for 1. Saturday morning, which saw an upturn in the weather, brought a crowd of 6,000 to the ground. The sunshine brought a remarkable change in the batting of Lancashire who ended their innings with 188 runs on the board. Nottingham replied with 23 for 4 as the game ended in a draw.

The Liverpool Club, taking advantage of the temporary ground improvements, hastily arranged a contest with the Free Foresters. The visitors, still active to-day, had been formed in 1856 by the Rev W K R Bedford at Sutton Coldfield. The team was so named because the players hailed from an area of England that lay between the Forest of Arden (Warwickshire) and the Forest of Neddlewood (Staffordshire). They were a wandering club whose membership was limited to players born, or living, in the Midland Counties of England. They were, for many years, the only amateur club to feature in the first class fixture list. The visit of the Free Foresters, much to the disappointment of the committee, attracted only a small crowd most of whom were leisured gentlemen.

31st July - Liverpool & District v The Australians

The Australians had already beaten Lancashire at Old Trafford when they arrived at Aigburth to take on the Liverpool and District XI. The home side despite their title contained five players who were based in Manchester. The visitors, captained by Bill Murdoch, featured Frederick (The Demon) Spofforth in their line up along with Charlie Bannerman. Murdoch won the toss and decided to bat.

The tourists, who made an unsteady start, were on 37 for 4 when George Griffin joined Irish born Tom Horan at the crease. The two players then put on 115 before Horan was caught off the bowling of John Crossland. The Australians went on to make a total of 240 runs in their first innings. The Liverpool side, despite a half century from A G Steel, scored just 112 in reply and were forced to accept the "follow on". Hopes of a quick Australian victory were dashed by the heavy rain that washed out all of the play on the second day of the match.

The Liverpool side, now with no hope of victory, was all out for 137 leaving the Australians needing to score10 runs in the eight minutes that remained of the game. This they failed to achieve and the game ended in a draw. (The Australia team, later in the season, beat England in the world's first test match at Oval. This victory gave birth, indirectly, to the present day Ashes series.)

There was a large turnout for the Liverpool Cricket Club AGM that was held in the Assembly Rooms in the centre of Liverpool. Many of the members, while optimistic of the future, complained of the imbalance between the numbers of county games played at Aigbuth in relation to the number played at Old Trafford. The 'Lions Share' had by far, been allocated to Manchester, while Liverpool, the largest town in the county, had received only a single fixture. Mr T D Hornby was detailed to attend the next County meeting at Old Trafford and plead for a greater share of the lucrative county matches to be diverted in the direction of Liverpool. Nevertheless, when the County fixtures were made known, Aigburth had been allocated just one game. This was to be played in July against Gloucestershire.

The impending cricket season meanwhile was awaited with great anticipation by all concerned with the sport in Liverpool. A local journalist, writing for the Liverpool Courier, looked forward to the occasion and waxed lyrical about his forthcoming visit to the Aigburth ground.

"The Thrushes of Aigburth betoken the near approach of "the season" at the paradise of English Cricket and, notwithstanding the difficulties of the times attending the return journey, it is truly pleasant to spend an afternoon amidst the delightful scenery of the charming suburb."

The public transport problem to which our lyrical friend referred was high on the agenda when the club committee next met at Aigburth. The secretary, in the hope of alleviating this problem, wrote to the regional headquarters of the Cheshire Lines at Liverpool Central Station. He requested that the passengers who alighted at Mersey Road Station, be given a more convenient access to the Liverpool cricket ground. The Railway Company, quick to reply, agreed to cut a row of steps in the embankment at the eastern end of the down platform. A special footpath was then laid to enable the public to reach the ground near the bottom of Riverside Road where they could enter the ground by turnstile. This was, at the time, the only way in to the ground as access was denied by way of the members' enclosure. The only other way of reaching the location from the centre of Liverpool was, if not by private carriage, the horse drawn tram service which terminated at the beginning of Aigburth Road. Those passengers who did not wish to walk had to complete their journey by the horse drawn omnibus service that operated between the Dingle and Garston. This arrangement operated until 1902 when a single electric tramline was laid between Aigburth Vale and Garston Village.

Mersey Road Railway Station later renamed Aigburth

Liverpool Ramblers AFC

The origins of this old, but little known, soccer club can be found amongst the sons of the leading commercial gentlemen of Liverpool. Many prominent family names such as Earle, Gladstone and Hornby are listed in the early membership. They were formed in 1882 and began playing matches behind the Aigburth Hotel before moving across the road to play on the cricket field. Ramblers, during the formative years, proved to be the mainstay of local soccer and were the first team to represent Liverpool in the FA Cup. They remained at Aigburth for two seasons before relocating at the rural north end of Merseyside. They later played at several locations before finally in 1937 settling at their present home in Crosby.

Today they play only club fixtures and are the oldest surviving amateur football team on Merseyside. They were the first team ever to use a goal net and the first to take soccer to Dublin. They are also the oldest club in the world who has never taken part in a league match of any description. Liverpool Ramblers will celebrate their 125th anniversary in 2007.

International Soccer

In 1882 the Football Association were searching the north of England in the hopes of finding a suitable location at which to stage the forthcoming International match between England and Ireland. They turned for help to Liverpool Ramblers AFC who promptly recommended the ground at Aigburth. The committee of Liverpool Cricket Club agreed to stage the match. The executive wasted no time in setting out their plans to accommodate the large crowd of people who were expected to attend this most prestigious event. They decided to mark out the playing pitch on the far side of the ground between the cricket strip and the railway cuttings. A reserved enclosure was constructed along the Aigburth Road side of the pitch that was approached, by means of a duckboard, directly from the pavilion. Hoardings were placed around the three remaining sides of the appointed area. An assortment of flat decked wagons, collected from around the district, were wheeled in and placed around the pitch to provide extra standing accommodation for the spectators. Goalposts, appropriate to the occasion, were set in place. A strong wire rope, to complete the setting, was drawn around the periphery to protect the field of play. The Liverpool committee, their task accomplished, now waited for the big day to arrive.

February 23rd 1883, was the day on which the match was played. The weather was cold but the brilliant sunshine gave grandeur to the occasion. Many fashionable people filled the reserved section while the railway side displayed a mass of spectators. The playing surface, prepared by George Ubsdall, was in perfect condition as the kick off time approached. The crowd, as the players left the pavilion, numbered around three thousand people. The teams were then summoned to their respective positions, and the play commenced.

The match that followed was a rather one sided affair that was, as expected, won by England. The host nation scored three times in each half to win the game, 6-0. Both teams, later that evening, dined at the Bears Paw Restaurant in Liverpool. The Irish team then caught the overnight ferry back to Belfast.

1883

The 1883 cricket season began with the regular fixture against Dingle. This game was then followed by a selection of club matches that preceded the much awaited visit of Gloucestershire.

Extra facilities were set in place for the comfort of the spectators, and a game with the Free Foresters was arranged to prelude the event. The weather sadly proved to be unfavourable.

The heavy rain which fell quickly saturated the new Aigburth ground and rendered it unfit to host the fixture and it was decided, at the eleventh hour, to transfer the game to Old Trafford. The cancellation was a big disappointment to the local cricket lovers who had looked forward to the appearance of W G Grace at the Liverpool ground. The local press, who thundered against this injustice, forced the Liverpool Club to issue a statement. They informed the public that the choice was *"theirs alone"* and that the County Committee had *"no voice whatsoever in the decision"*. The game was eventually played at Old Trafford. There was little else other than club fixtures seen on the Aigburth ground that Summer before Autumn brought the season to an end.

1884

This season got underway with the annual visit of Dingle. There then followed a succession of fixtures against clubs from Lancashire before the ground featured a week of first class cricket. The Australians, who had been in the North for two weeks, had already played out a draw with Lancashire at Old Trafford. The tourists then played a game against the North of England before heading over to the Mersey seaport.

23rd June Liverpool & District v Australia

The second visit of the Australians produced a game of cricket that was, for tension and excitement, to go down in local folklore and always be remembered by the people who were fortunate enough to be present. The Liverpool side opened the batting and, thanks to a fine knock by A G Steel (72), scored 213 in their first innings. The tourists were then bowled out for 140 runs before the proceedings were interrupted by rain. The Australian captain Bill Murdoch, now turned to the medium pace bowling of Harry Boyle and Eugene Palmer who dismissed the home side for 54 runs. The tourists, needing 128 to win, were guided home by the batting of Murdoch. The Australian captain, in a last wicket stand with Boyle, won the game with minutes to spare.

17th July Lancashire v Surrey

It was the first time the Metropolitan players had been seen in Liverpool since their appearance on the old Spekefield ground. The match drew a good crowd as the home side featured four of the Steel brothers. Lancashire lost the toss and was requested to field. The visitors, who made a poor start, were indebted to the middle order innings of John Shuter. The Surrey captain, who stabilized his side, made 56 runs before his side was dismissed for 163 runs. Lancashire, in reply, was 102/7 at the close of play. The home side offered little resistance and were all out for 126 during the morning session. Surrey, who began their second innings well, collapsed, (along with the pitch) from 71/3 to 95 all out leaving Lancashire to score 133 to win. Batting on a difficult wicket they made a gallant effort before failing in their attempt. They were bowled out for 103 and lost the game by 29 runs.

1885

As the cricket season approached the greensward at Aigburth was in a faultless condition thanks to the diligent care of the groundsman, George Ubsdall. Mr Ubsdall was born in Southampton in 1845 and made his debut for Hampshire at the age of nineteen. He played fifteen times in all for his native county, the last of which was against Lancashire at Old Trafford. He later acquired the job of club professional at Childwall before joining the ground staff at Liverpool. The environment at Aigburth must have been to his fondness as he spent the rest of his life in the area and died in Garston in 1905.

The club committee meanwhile decided to employ the services of two professional bowlers from Nottingham, William and **Alfred Price**, for the benefit of the members. Their task was to bowl against and coach the members and play when required for the club. They could live in huts at the side of the ground and any tips they received were paid to them in food, not cash, a form of payment that continued for many years.

The approaching fixture list, published in the local press, announced that two hitherto unseen teams were to be expected on the Aigburth ground in the course of the coming season. The students of Dublin University, along with the Castle Club from Nottingham, did indeed appear on the Aigburth ground later that summer. The highlight of the season, however, was the return visit of Surrey.

16th June Lancashire v Surrey

This match was restricted to just two eventful days on account of the weather. The visitors won the toss and after just over two hours of play, were all out for a score of 117 runs. The home side in reply, had reached 191 for 9 when R. Pilling joined J. Briggs at the crease. The two players then made history on the Aigburth ground. They fashioned a record last wicket partnership of 173 runs before Briggs, with the score standing at 394, was dismissed just twelve runs short of his double century. The visitors, for the loss of 5 wickets, were still 24 runs short of the Lancashire total when heavy rain washed out all hopes of play on the final day.

1st July Lancashire v Surrey

There was a large crowd waiting to greet the return of the Londoners as they took to the field followed by the opening batsmen of Lancashire. The home side, taking advantage of the excellent wicket, quickly piled on the runs. They batted well into the second day and acquired a total of 426 runs. The visitors, all out for 229, were forced to accept the 'follow on'. A G Steel now took centre stage. He returned bowling figures of 7 for 95 as the London side were dismissed for a total of 168 runs. Lancashire won the game by an innings and 27 runs.

1886
16th July Liverpool & District v Australians

This game brought the welcome return of the Australian touring team to the Aigburth Ground. The heavy rain, which made play impossible on day one, had abated on the morning of day two. The tourists, who won the all important toss, batted first and made a total of 119. Liverpool & District then struggled against the bowling of Turner and Worrall who had the home side all back in the pavilion with just 70 runs on the board. George Bonner with 46, was the top scorer as the Australians hit

150 in their second innings. The wicket had cut up badly when the home side, needing 199 to win, began their second innings. The bowling of Charlie (Terror) Turner again proved too much for the home side. The New South Wales bowler, backed up by Jack Worrell, returned figures of 6 for 36. Only H. B. Steel, with 31 runs, offered any resistance as the tourists won the game by 130 runs.

1887

The year 1887 was to be a special one in the life of the British nation as their reigning monarch, Queen Victoria, was to celebrate her Golden Jubilee. The Liverpool Club's fixture list, to honour the occasion, displayed a total of 56 games that were to be executed by the cricket section during the months of summer at various levels.

The Gentlemen players of Canada paid a visit to Aigburth along with Cheshire and the newly formed County XI of Warwickshire. The third week of June was designated as a period of particular celebration that was to be called "Jubilee Week". It included two first class cricket matches amongst other celebrations.

Mr Freay who was the Assistant Secretary and part time steward gave notice because of ill-health and moved to the Canary Isles to manage the Hotel Metropole in Las Palmas. Three years later the club went on their first overseas tour and stayed at the hotel. They played eight matches and won all of them. Two years later they returned to the island this time taking a tennis team with them.

20th June Lancashire and Oxford University

The visitors, who batted first, scored a total of 273 runs to which Lancashire in reply were all out for 164. The home side, forced to follow on, recovered to end the second day on a score of 271 for the loss of 8 wickets. A crowd of 5,000 were present on the first two days thanks to warm and sunny weather, but the skies were dull and threatening as the players took to the field on the final day. The crowd, influenced by this fact, was considerably reduced in numbers as Lancashire ended their innings on 284 leaving the visitors to score 175 for victory. The Dark Blues then suffered an unaccountable collapse as Lancashire bowled them out for just 58 runs to win the match by 117 runs.

23rd June Liverpool & District XI v Yorkshire

The match, which attracted 2,000 people, was a high scoring game. The home team consisted of eight local amateurs plus three professional bowlers. The visitors were captained by Louis Hall. Yorkshire, batting second, was in a strong position at the end of the first day. They trailed the home side, by one run for the loss of five wickets. The home side, which dismissed Yorkshire for 248, recovered and was 242/8 at the close of play on the second day. The home side, all out for 259, then bowled out Yorkshire to win the game by 38 runs. This game brought the festival week to an end. The Jubilee year, a great success, was one that would always be remembered at Aigburth as the season drew slowly to an end.

1888
2nd July Liverpool & District v Australia

The Liverpool XI was again made up of eight local players plus three professional bowlers while Spofforth was missing from the visiting team. The match was restricted to two days due to rain, which was to prove time enough for an Australian victory. Leading, after the first innings by 39 runs the tourists ended the day on 67/2. Resuming the next day the Australians were all out for 150 leaving the home team to score 200 runs to win. The Liverpool side, all out for 69, lost the match by 130 runs.

On July 23rd 1888 the Gentlemen of Liverpool played host to the Parsees touring team from India. The visitors, in 1886, were the first Asian cricket team to have ever visited England. They were all followers of the Zoroastrian faith who had left Persia in 745AD when the country was invaded by the Arabs. They then spent many years farming while practising their faith in India. In the 17th century, encouraged by British land grants and, promises of religious freedom, the Parsees settled in and around the City of Bombay. Bombay, following the first Indian War of Independence, reverted to the crown of Great Britain in 1857. The setting was an ideal site for a seaport and the British made much of this. They improved the existing harbour facilities and built shipyards and textile mills. The Parsee community, now numbering around 100,000, prospered under the rule of the British and quickly embraced their national game of cricket.

The Parsee team who toured England 1886

The Parsees began the batting and scored 51 runs in their first innings The Gentlemen of Liverpool responded with a good opening partnership by Roper and Kemble who scored a combined total of 77 runs. A score of 35 from G Bird then saved Liverpool from a collapse as they were all out for 130 runs. The visitors, who batted much better on the second day, were again dismissed for a total of 134 runs. The Gentlemen of Liverpool, needing 56 runs to win, achieved this score for the loss of 5 wickets.

26th July Lancashire v Gloucestershire

Wickets tumbled in abundance on the day the legendary W. G. Grace made his first appearance on the Liverpool ground. The visitors began the day well by dismissing the home side for 108 runs only to be bowled out themselves for just 33 runs. (W. G. was bowled by Barlow for 4.) The wickets continued to fall when Lancashire returned to the crease as they ended the day on 89/6. Lancashire, when they recommenced the next day, added just eight runs leaving Gloucestershire to score 173 to win. The wickets however, continued to tumble. W. G. (again bowled by Barlow) was the top scorer with 16 as the visitors were dismissed for 56 runs. Lancashire won the match by 116 runs.

1889

In the summer of 1889 the district of Aigburth was at the centre of a famous murder trial that was to rock the nation to its very foundations. James Maybrick, a member of Liverpool Cricket Club, was alleged to have been poisoned by his American wife Florence. The couple, who had two children, lived in a large house that overlooked the cricket ground. The mansion, formerly called "Battlecrease House", still stands to-day. It was from here, via Walton Jail, that Florence Maybrick was taken to stand trial for her life at St Georges Hall in Liverpool.

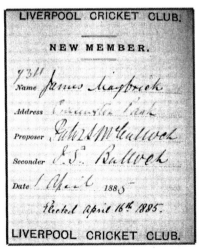

The accepted membership of James Maybrick

The proceedings which lasted several days, captured the

imagination of the English speaking world. Each day, as certain evidence came to light, the size of the crowd began to increase around the court room. Rumours, relating to the private life of James Maybrick, began to circulate amongst the population of Liverpool. Mr Maybrick, as it was later proved, was addicted to arsenic. He also had children to a second woman in the Whitechapel area of London. The Liverpool public sensed an injustice was taking place within their midst and started to make their feelings known. Nevertheless Florence, after being found guilty of murder, was sentenced to hang at Walton Jail.

James Maybrick

The waiting crowd, around three thousand in number, howled with disapproval when the verdict was made public. Shouts of encouragement greeted Florence as she boarded the prison van and left St Georges Hall under a police escort. This was in total contrast to the reception that greeted the departure of the presiding official, Justice James Fitzjames Stephen. His Lordship, when boarding his carriage, was greeted with manifestations of the utmost contempt as he began his journey back to his temporary lodging at Newsham Park. The crowd eventually dispersed peacefully. Florence Maybrick meanwhile, languished in her cell at Walton Jail.

Public condemnation on both sides of the Atlantic now began to come to the aid of the American lady. Florence it was alleged, had suffered a gross miscarriage of justice. Nowhere were these feelings felt more than in her adopted home town of Liverpool. The authorities, fearing violent social disorder, now began to have second thoughts. The Home Secretary, with the consent of the Monarch, repealed the death penalty and reduced the sentence to that of 15 years imprisonment. It was also decided to move Florence to a prison in the Surrey town of Woking.

She was transported, again by prison van, to Lime Street Station. The diminutive "Southern Belle", wearing her prison uniform, was given warm salutations of encouragement by the many people present, as she crossed the station concourse and boarded the waiting train. The crowd then watched in silence as the London Express drew slowly away from the platform. Florence would never see Aigburth or her two children again.

She completed her sentence at Woking prison from where, following her release in 1904, she was admitted to a convent in the Cornish town of Truro. She remained there for six months. Her mother, Baroness Von Roques, arrived in England and escorted Florence back to her native America. She eventually settled near the small town of South Kent in Connecticut, after first living in Chicago. Florence Maybrick, in the later years of her life, became very reclusive. She was however, adopted by the pupils from the local school who looked after her until, aged 79, she died in 1941. She is buried in South Kent cemetery.

Florence, Elizabeth, nee Chandler, Maybrick 1861-1941.
A Lady Subscriber to Liverpool Cricket Club

1890

As the 1890s approached, Liverpool Cricket Club began to develop regular fixtures with neighbouring clubs such as Northern, Sefton and Birkenhead Park, which would in time replace long day trips to such places as Eccles, Manchester and Leyland. The demise of the Liverpool & District Club who played their last game in 1894, restricted the first class games (without the Australian tourists) to one county game a year. Touring sides, such as Fettes Lorettos and Harrow Wanderers, continued to visit Aigburth but top quality fixtures remained in short supply. If the location was to consistently attract a large number of spectators, an improvement in the amount of county games was clearly needed. The local newspapers, who thought the allocation unfair, were clearly on the side of the Liverpool Club.

"In noticing the prospects of cricket for Liverpool and its district, it is much to be deplored that the Lancashire executive on their part deny the seaport the one county fixture which was yearly doled out to it. Such vandalism is unexplainable. One thing is certain; it is not done in the true interest of the game. It has been suggested that £ s.d. was the principal motive power which moved the management of Lancashire county cricket in their unjust conduct towards Liverpool; but more probably it was one of jealousy, and if this isolation of the seaport from participating in county matches is persisted in, then the Liverpool club and public should endeavour by some means or other to retaliate on the Manchester clique for robbing them of one of the carnivals of the year. With this exception, the match list of the titular club of the city is much the same as previously. Mr Kewley, the Hon. Secretary of the club, has arranged for the Yorkshire County team to play a three day match at Aigburth against Liverpool & District in May, and it is to be hoped the weather will be more favourable for the occasion than it was last year. This will be followed later on by visits from Fettes-Lorettos and Harrow Wanderers. Wigan and Stockport have been eliminated from this year's list, but a fresh fixture (Castleton) appears: while the meeting between the Gentlemen of Manchester and the Gentlemen of Liverpool takes place at Grassendale. A week in June and another in August are devoted to the Lawn Tennis Tournament and the Grand Archery meeting respectively. So altogether the attractions at Aigburth this

season will be both plentiful and varied, and it is to be hoped the public will appreciate the fact by giving the pretty grounds a visit, especially as in the majority of instances they are free of charge."
(Liverpool Daily Post, April 19th 1890).

"*In the absence of a county match at Aigburth, the local programme is scarcely so strong as in previous years : but while the withdrawal of the fixture is deeply to be regretted, the best thanks of the community are due to Mr Dunlop and Mr Kewley for their eloquent pleading on behalf of the "good old town". It is a well known fact that from the first the county committee regarded Liverpool with disfavour, and year after year the "geographical" argument has been advanced, finally with success, and now, maybe, no further concession will be made for many a year to come. It was the same with football: but of course the inevitable must be accepted with becoming humility. The gentlemen of the Liverpool club have the power and the will to institute a new order of things, and if the residents of the district will condescend to recognise and give their generous efforts, a new and prosperous era in the matter of local cricket will be inaugurated, a consummation which, it will be admitted, is most devoutly to be wished for. The natural attractions of Aigburth are of such surpassing beauty that no more charming enclosure exists throughout the length and breadth of the land and it is therefore to be hoped that the claims of the leading club will not be overlooked. As in the former years, local clubs have been generously dealt with, there scarcely being an organisation possessing the slightest claim to merit that will not be afforded the opportunity of the concession on the greensward at Aigburth.*"
(Liverpool Courier, 26th April, 1890.)

This was not, despite local pessimism, the end of county cricket at Liverpool and seven county matches took place between then and the turn of the century.

To add to the leisure activities of the members a quoits team was set up but there are no records to show that this was ever a spectator sport. It is still enjoyed by a small group to this day.

1896

The Club agreed to rent out the lower ground but not the pavilion to Liverpool Rugby Club during the winter months for the sum of £15 on the condition that they had only one team and finished by the end of January. Their request to charge members for entry to the ground on match days was refused by the LCC as this was against club rules. This agreement had to be renegotiated each year, once being refused following the sub – letting of the pitch by the Rugby Club to Liverpool Ladies Hockey Club without permission from the cricket secretary.

1897

The Club was to host their first county hockey match between Lancashire and Middlesex and it was this year that the committee was to appoint their first full time steward, Mr Hillsdon for a wage of £2 per week.

Sadly this year saw the death of Liverpool Cricket Club's first President the 4th Earl of Sefton leaving a vacancy to be considered.

During these latter years the pavilion was finally finished with showers and an extra changing room on the top floor. Commercialisation dawned, and the perimeter railings were replaced with a substantial brick wall to encourage spectators to pay to watch the games.

1898

Decisions made in this year included Mr. Charles Langdon elected President and a croquet set was purchased for the use of members. This is the only sport mentioned that does not continue to be played to the present day.

Brief consideration was given to the facility of a tea wagon inside the ground but it was not thought 'in keeping' and was dismissed. After all members could enjoy refreshment in the pavilion!

Application was made once again by the Liverpool (Rugby) Football Club for the use of the ground during the winter months up to the end of February, for not only their first team but their recent addition of a 2nd side. Balancing the need for the money this brought into the Club against the wear and tear on the ground, whilst agreement was reached, the proviso was made that should the LCC Secretary consider the ground unfit all games would be stopped.

1899

As previously recorded the Club had taken over the use of the ground on the far side of the railway line, known as 'The Lower Ground', by now enclosed partially by railings and otherwise by a brick wall still standing to the present day. The promised pavilion was eventually built but subsequently demolished following a fire. These facilities were further improved with the laying on of water at a cost of £23 to the club.

Although in April of this year the Old Girls Hockey Club was granted permission to hold a ladies sports day on the original ground it was only on the new site that the rugby club was allowed to play in the forthcoming years.

Slowly things were moving forward and for the first time a

woman was allowed to join as a Lady Subscriber without a male relative being a member. It is not recorded whether this event had any bearing on the fact that in May of this same year a Croquet section was formed.

The short sighted (or fearful?) committee allowed schoolboy sons of members to join the Club but they were not afforded full membership rights and consequently not allowed to benefit from the expertise of the professionals or use the upstairs changing rooms.

Further expense was sanctioned this year for two new stands on the top ground at £40 each, with a request that they be built on wheels. Today what seems a very strange order is easily explained in that 'stands' at this time consisted of a sloping wooden platform and not the elaborate seating arrangements that can now be enjoyed in comfort at many sports grounds.

CHAPTER 3

Turbulent Years - 1900 to 1939

So it was the year ended and the church bells of Liverpool rang the old year out and welcomed in the new century. The Monarch, Queen Victoria, was in the sixty third year of her reign over the largest empire on the planet. The nation had become embroiled in a war with the Boer farmers in South Africa and thousands of troops were embarking from Liverpool, in order to join the conflict. RMS Cymric, a liner with the White Star Line, sailed from Canada Dock early on 1st January. She was carrying men of the Royal Field Artillery along with a battalion of the Gloucestershire Regiment all of whom were bound for Cape Town. Many members of the Liverpool Cricket Club took part in the Boer War and some of them lost their lives. However hostilities of a different kind, threatened the serenity at Aigburth.

1900

There was an air of anxiety prevailing at the club when the first AGM of the new century took place in the Assembly Rooms. The enemy of old, the railway company, was once again threatening the cricket boundaries. It had come to the attention of the membership that the Cheshire Lines Committee were planning to widen the railway cutting and lay another two lines, in order to provide an express link with Manchester. This of course could only be done at the expense of the second cricket field. (We know today that this planned expansion did not come to fruition but it must have been an area of great concern to the members of old.)

In keeping with the 'gentlemanly behavour' displayed at this time it was deemed unnecessary to go to the expense of sight screens but to rely on the use of a rope to prevent the movement of spectators behind the bowlers arms and therefore in the batsman's sight.

The club once again expanded the sporting facilities available to members with the introduction of the gentle game of bowls. Still enjoyed to this day it is afforded separate recognition in this History of Liverpool Cricket Club.

To add to the enjoyment of non-member spectators a tender of £20 was accepted from Mr Rigby to sell refreshments outside of the pavilion.

A visiting theatrical group, in Liverpool to perform 'Charlie's Aunt', was allowed to use the sporting facilities of the Club for the duration of their visit.

During this year the Club's second president Mr C. Langton died.

The committee paid compliment to Teddy Roper for the fostering care he had displayed towards Liverpool Cricket Club thus earning them world wide fame. No visiting team, be it from Australia, Africa or Asia, were allowed to come and go without having given the Liverpool & District side an opportunity to test their cricketing abilities.

The meeting was next informed of the impending departure of Alan G Steele from Liverpool. The veteran all rounder, arguably the Club's finest ever player, was leaving his birthplace in order to practise law in London. Mr. Steele, upon his departure, was made a life member of the Liverpool Cricket Club.

The position of Head Groundsman was given to Francis H. Goodwin, one of the ground bowlers. Frank Goodwin coming from a large cricketing family had on occasions, before coming to Aigburth, fielded a team entirely of relatives.

Moving his family into the lodge his income was £75 a year plus free gas, coal and rent, along with the right to sell goods from a shop on the ground.

Born in Rainhill in 1866, Mr. Goodwin first gained knowledge of cricket while playing for the local Asylum where he was training to be a gardener. He later played for St Helens before joining the Liverpool ground staff in 1894. Later that year he made his debut for Lancashire in a friendly fixture against Derbyshire. He was selected to play in the next two county matches against Surrey and Kent respectively, but was given no opportunity to show his outstanding talent as a bowler against Surrey and refused to play against Kent unless he could bowl. Consequently he was never selected again.

Mr. Goodwin then devoted himself to his club and went on most of the club's school tours. He did however go on to coach other players who would later distinguish themselves in the service of the Red Rose County.

He was also a talented violinist and played at many venues in Liverpool.

At the age of 55 he decided to retire and take the less arduous post of steward at the Elder Dempster sports ground on Aigburth Road.

In 1931 he died of blood poisoning from a carbuncle at the age of 65. The respect in which he was held can be judged by the number of dignitaries who attended his funeral at St Anne's Parish Church. He is buried in Allerton Cemetery.

His daughter Freda was the first lady to be an official scorer in a county match officiating between Cheshire and Glamorganshire in 1920.

***Aigburth Road during the early part
of the Twentieth Century.***

Back on the home front meanwhile, the start of the cricket season was greeted with delight by many of the soldiers who were home on leave from the African War. The fixture with Preston, following the demise of Dingle, now and for several years to come, marked the opening of the cricket season at Aigburth. H. B. Steel scored the first runs of the new century and the game ended in a draw. The rest of the summer was, following a short period of local fixtures, to prove the most eventful yet to be seen on the Aigburth ground.

Played on the Ground of the Liverpool C.C., Aigburth, September 7th, 1901.

LIVERPOOL.

	First Innings.		Second Innings.
1 H B Steel	b Burrough	14	
2 E E Steel	not out	114	
3 H G Garnett	c W ... ernie b Pilling	18	
4 J Graham. Jun	c Shutt b Pilling	26	
5 A F Spooner	b Burrough	9	
6 A L Melly	not out	19	
7 W Hilton			
8 F M Garnett			
9 F Edmondson			
10 O M Kinnear			
11 Goodwin			
	Wds 4 bys 7 lbs 1 nb	12	Wds bys lb nb
	Total for 4 wkts... 212		Total...

FALL OF THE WICKETS.

1	2	3	4	5	6	7	8	9	10	1	2	3	4	5	6	7	8	9	10
20	53	119	156																

ANALYSIS OF THE BOWLING.

	First Innings.				Second Innings.			
	O.	M.	R.	W.	O.	M.	R.	W.
Rev J Burrough	18	1	78	2				
Shutt	16	6	67	0				
E S Pilling	11	1	52	2				
T Routledge	1	0	3	0				

NORTHERN.

	First Innings.		Second Innings.
1 Rev J Burrough	b Goodwin	19	
2 W D Lloyd	c Hilton b E E Steel	2	
3 R K Fernie	lbw b Goodwin	1	
4 T Routledge	c Edmondson b Goodwin	0	
5 W Fraser	c and b Goodwin	0	
6 E L Pick	not out	32	
7 Shutt	b Goodwin	0	
8 E S Pilling	b Goodwin	0	
9 G W Fraser	b Goodwin	1	
10 W K Fernie	st Garnett b Goodwin	0	
11 F W Boucher	c Kinnear b Goodwin	7	
	Wds bys 4 lbs 1 nb	5	Wds bys lbs nb
	Total... 67		Total...

FALL OF THE WICKETS.

1	2	3	4	5	6	7	8	9	10	1	2	3	4	5	6	7	8	9	10
15	16	16	20	25	25	29	29												

ANALYSIS OF THE BOWLING.

	First Innings.				Second Innings.			
	O.	M.	R.	W.	O.	M.	R.	W.
E E Steel	18	7	27	1				
Goodwin	19·4	14	16	9				
W Hilton	4	1	8	0				
F M Garnett	2	0	11	0				

Score sheet from 1901 – note the 'class distinction'

between 'gentlemen' and 'professionals',

the professionals were not afforded the courtesy of initials!

The first fixture list of the new century revealed not one but two county games allocated to Aigburth. Both matches were won by Lancashire. Warwickshire arrived in May and, in two days, were soundly beaten by 10 wickets, while a worse fate awaited Somerset. When they arrived on 2nd July Lancashire, thanks to some excellent batting by Archie MacLaren, beat their West Country opponents, by an innings and 132 runs.

Later that year Aigburth played host to a side of colonial cricketers from the West Indies, who were on a tour of England. The match, played against a Liverpool and District XI, was not given first class status. It did however, produce some excellent cricket. The tourists were to have been captained by Aucher Warner, the brother of Pelham, but, due to an attack of sunstroke, he missed the match and Stanley Sproston took his place. Also in the team was Lebrun Costantine the father of Sir Leary Constantine. A feature of the first day's play was the excellent batting of Stanley Sproston who, without a blemish in his batting, made 118 runs. He was the last man out as the visitors ended their first innings with 265 runs on the board. At the close of play the home side was 98 for the loss of one wicket. The weather then broke. Heavy rain that fell throughout the night increased to a downpour flooding the already soaked ground. A thunderstorm was next on the agenda with the flashes of lightning having a pyrotechnic effect on the trees and neatly laid shrubs around the ground. The playing field soon resembled a lake with little tufts of grass showing up here and there, while the howling wind rippled the flowing ground with waves. Play was abandoned for the day but the pitch, amazingly, was playable the next morning. When play recommenced the home side ended their innings 47 runs behind the visitors who, declaring their second innings at 5 pm, left the home side to score 172 runs for victory. This they failed to do and the game ended in a draw.

In all, 55 county matches were played by Lancashire at the Aigburth ground between 1900 and the start of World War 2. Many famous players were to appear on the ground taking part in a variety of exciting matches. Giving an account of all these games would overpower a local history publication but there follows a few matches that may be noteworthy.

1901

Following the election of the Club's third President Mr H. H.Hornby it was decided for posterity to place portraits of all the Past Presidents on view in the pavilion. There is no record that this was ever achieved at the time but was finally undertaken and completed in 2006.

The years and weather having taken their toll it was necessary to replace the covers of the entrance turnstiles, originally built in leather with more substantial wooden structures.

Giving first credence to the title of this history the committee found it necessary to take steps to prevent nursemaids from sitting with their charges in front of the main stand.

Today members can see a plan of the grounds of LCC between 1829 and 1887 on the wall of the committee room thanks to the presentation this year, by Mr. A L. Melly the great uncle of one George Melly, jazz singer and raconteur, well known to many current members.

Records made at the time, possibly kept brief for discretion, relate that it was felt necessary to relieve the Steward Mr Hillsdon of his post due to his behaviour on the night of the polo club dinner. Speculation can only be made as to whether this incident resulted in the Club never considering extending the facilities to include water sports!

1902

21ˢᵗ July Lancashire v Middlesex

Unrelenting rain prevented any play on the first day when Middlesex made their first visit to Liverpool. The visitors, led by Pelham Warner, included Australian star Albert Trott in their line up. Middlesex batted slightly better than the home side and built up a first innings lead of 52 runs. Lancashire was then all out for 178 giving them a lead of 125 runs. As time ran out for Middlesex, the game ended in a draw.

Liverpool Ladies Hockey Team was allowed to play on the lower ground for five pounds a season up until the end of February.

The tennis section employed their first professional, a Mr Marshell from Paris, at a cost of three pounds a week and his fare from Paris.

1903

30ᵗʰ July Lancashire v Gloucestershire

A record opening partnership for Lancashire was set on this day by Reggie Spooner and Archie Maclaren. Opening the match they scored 368 runs between them before Spooner was out having made 168 runs. Maclaren went on to make 204 as Lancashire ended the day on 474/3. The game however was spoilt by the weather. Play did not resume until after 5 pm the next day as Lancashire declared their innings on 474/3. Gloucester, in reply, ended the day on 49/5. Next day, with Gloucester all out for 135, the match was abandoned as a draw.

Reginald Herbert Spooner

Born on 21st October 1880 in Litherland, Reggie Spooner was possibly the most stylish batsman ever to have been born on Merseyside. The son of an Anglican Clergyman he was educated at Marlborough College before returning to live with his family in the rectory at Much Woolton. His style of play, along with brother Archie, was nurtured by Frank Goodwin. The Liverpool professional spent many hours at Much Woolton and, under his watchful eye, the two brothers quickly developed into first class cricketers. Reggie however, was to prove the most successful and his exploits were soon to be reported by the local press. ...
"Quite recently against Bootle at the Hawthorne Road, Master Reginald Spooner, who by the way is a son of Canon Spooner of Much Woolton, created quite a thrill of admiration by his superb play. For so young a player he is a resolute and powerful batsman and one of the best boys at Marlborough this season. He is an apt pupil, and has already done ample justice to his private and painstaking coach, Frank Goodwin, of the Liverpool Club."

It was on the 17th August 1899, at Lords where he made his first class debut, scoring 46 for Lancashire in their match against Middlesex. He was, for a while, absent from the game after being wounded on active service during the Boer War. He played ten times for England making his debut at Old Trafford against Australia in 1905. He went on to play 237 first class cricket matches the last of which was for the MCC against Yorkshire at Scarborough. Reggie Spooner, in later years, became land agent for Lord Londesborough and died on 2 October 1961, at Lincoln.

*The Reverend Archdeacon Spooner pictured
with Frank Goodwin at Aigburth.*

1907

20th June Lancashire v Sussex

The first visit of the legendary Charles Burgess Fry to Aigburth was awaited with great anticipation by the cricket lovers amongst the population of Liverpool. Rain however, held up the start and the play began on day two. Everton football players Jack Sharp and Harry Makepeace who were in the Lancashire line up, added to the attraction and brought a large crowd to witness the proceedings. The home side won the game with ease. The visitors, chasing a Lancashire first innings score of 116, were all out for 78 runs. The home side then scored 298 in their second innings leaving Sussex to score 337 runs to win. Their reply proved to be poor in the extreme. The classic batting of C. B. Fry, who made a duck in both innings, was absent in the match. The south coast side was all out for a total of just 29 runs in just fifty minutes. The margin of victory, by over 300 runs, was the largest yet to be achieved by the county side at Liverpool and was to contrast greatly with the forthcoming visit of Nottinghamshire.

22nd August Lancashire v Nottinghamshire

When they arrived at Aigburth the east midland side demonstrated why they had already won the county championship. The visitors, who won the toss, elected to bat first. Their innings was opened by George Gunn who was accompanied by the giant goalkeeper of Notts County AFC, Albert Iremonger. The Lancashire bowlers had a moderate success against the champions until Arthur Jones arrived at the crease. The England player hit 94 runs as his team ended their innings with a score of 250 runs. Lancashire, in reply, were 25 for 1 when bad light ended play on the first day. When play resumed Lancashire was bowled out in just forty minutes for a total of 82 runs and was forced to accept the "follow on". A worse performance then followed as the home side was bowled out for a meagre 37 runs. This is, to date, the lowest total to be made in an innings by Lancashire at Aigburth. Nottinghamshire won the match by an innings and 131 runs.

Jack Sharp

Jack Sharp belongs to that elite band of sportsmen who have represented England at both football and cricket. Born in Hereford in 1878 he was a football player with Aston Villa when on 8th June 1899, he made his cricketing debut for Lancashire. Chosen for his left arm bowling abilities, he delighted the Old Trafford crowd by scoring 57 runs while batting right handed against Surrey. He was an instant success in his initial season and represented Lancashire fifteen times. In September that year he left Aston Villa and signed for Everton making his debut against Sheffield United on the first day of the season. He was to prove to be a most popular player with the Goodison faithful appearing for the club in 342 league and cup games in which he scored 80 goals. He was twice chosen to play for England and was a member of the Everton FA Cup winning team of 1907. In 1909, while still at Everton, he retired from the game and later joined the board of directors at Goodison Park. His cricket career however was to last until 1925.

He was a firm favourite with the followers of Lancashire Cricket Club who much admired his sportsmanlike qualities. Although not a member of Liverpool Cricket Club, during the summer months he was often seen practising in the nets at

Aigburth having been given permission to use their facilities.

At the height of his career Jack Sharp played three times for England against Australia in the 1909 test series scoring a century in the 5th test at the Oval. He played a total of 518 games for Lancashire scoring 22,015 runs and taking 434 wickets. From 1923 to 1925 he captained Lancashire and made his last appearance at Aigburth against Sussex, in July 1925. He died in Wavertree on 28th January 1938.

Many people in Liverpool will remember his name from the sports' outfitters shop in the city centre.

Harry Makepeace

Harry Makepeace, like Jack Sharp, is of that small group of talented men to have represented England at both football and cricket. Born on 22nd August 1881 in Middlesbrough he moved to Liverpool while still a child. A gifted sportsman he signed for Everton in 1902 and was part of the Everton FA Cup winning team of 1907. He was a talented half back and was selected to play for England on four occasions. He played in 336 league and FA Cup matches in the Everton colours and scored 23 goals.

He was a fine right-handed batsman and a leg break bowler. He made his debut for Lancashire in July 1906 against Essex at Leyton where he opened the batting with Archie MacLean. Harry Makepeace, on the 1921 tour of Australia, played in four test matches and scored a century at Melbourne. His last appearance for the Red Rose County was, rather appropriately, at Aigburth, in a match in August 1930 against Middlesex. He played for Lancashire on 487 occasions scoring 25,207 runs and taking 42 wickets. He died in Bebington on 19th December 1952.

1908

In 1908 the Aigburth location, underwent several changes. An extra function suite, known as the Red Room, was added to the main building and the steps in front of the pavilion were replaced. A new covered stand was constructed on the western side of the playing field. The price of this work proved to be costly and forced the committee to solicit the financial support of the membership. The Liverpool Club also wrote to Old Trafford for support and was granted 10% of the revenue taken at the county games. These transactions raised a total of £354.

Over the next few years the committee continued to oversee improvements to the exciting facilities at Aigburth. The ladies pavilion was demolished and a superior one, complete with servants quarters, erected in its place. The building was fitted with all the conveniences conducive to modern living along with a covered balcony at the front. The lady hockey players, who used the building during the winter, were charged an annual rent of £10. The club's coffers meanwhile were beginning to show signs of strain.

Due to several seasons of bad weather attendances were very much in decline and certain employees were forced to take a cut in their wages. The number of professional players was cut and the two playing fields were hired out for various activities during the winter months. The number of cricket matches was also reduced and the lower ground was hired out to a local shipping company.

1909

Whilst not a memorable year for the cricketing fraternity, decisions were made regarding the other sports either already played at the club or emerging as popular pastimes. The piece of ground by the entrance gate, used by the quoits team, was requisitioned for a bowling green where it remains to this day and the Rugby Club became honorary members of LCC for the duration of the season. As most of the men were members of both clubs it did not affect many of them but it enabled the whole team to use the lower changing rooms instead of some having to suffer in a tent on the ground. This enabled them access to the washing facilities such as they were. A couple of barrels of water were supplied for all of them but whether hot or cold is not recorded. The upstairs changing rooms were still 'off limits'.

Adding to the expenses this year was the necessity to replace tablecloths and napkins (ladies and gentlemen for the use of) destroyed in a fire thought to have broken out in the laundry room on the ground floor.

1910

Whilst the Liverpool Cricket Club was a 'rich gentlemen's' club it was never a 'gentlemen's' rich club and the need for a covered stand posed the dilemma of 'how to pay for it'. The Rugby Club were first to offer the finance and rent it back to the Cricket Club who responded by meeting the cost and recuperating it by leasing it to the Rugby Club!

Using the negotiating table the Rugby Club sought and obtained a ten year tenure and for the first time they could plan their future without the worry that next year they may be elsewhere.

Due to ever increasing expenses and the need to stabilise the bank balance the lower ground was advertised for rent the following summer.

1911

Among the responses to this commercial enterprise was one from a hopeful farmer wanting to graze his sheep which was declined in favour of the terms offered by Elder Dempster Shipping Line. £20 per season for the ground, stand included, and 18 shillings for the groundsman to maintain the pitch in playing condition. The grass cuttings were to be sold to a local farmer for £5.

Despite the shortage of money, or maybe because of, this year saw the completion of the upper changing rooms and showers, and Mr Roper, the Club Secretary, was asked to agree to a reduction in his salary to £200 per annum (a reduction of £50). Of course being a gentleman of private means this created no hardship and the request was accepted.

Benevolent members now began to donate artifacts of sporting interest to the club, one being a photograph of the old rules of cricket by Mr A.L.Melly. Another being 'a picture' of the first rugby match played at LCC but whether a painting or a photograph goes unrecorded. Along with other such items these were stored for safekeeping but unfortunately do not survive to the present day.

Also donated was the book 'Lilley's 25 Years of Cricket'.

1912
1st August, Lancashire v South Africa

Inclement weather delayed the start of the game and it was turned 2 pm before the home side opened the batting. Lancashire, despite the lifeless pitch, reached a first innings total of 242. This was mainly due to an excellent score of 121 by Jack Sharp. Admirable bowling by Bill Huddleston, 7 for 42 then put the home side in a strong position as the visitors were all out for 124. Lancashire, on the final morning, ended their second innings with 151 runs on the board. The South Africans, needing 279 to win, now faced a hopeless task. On a difficult wicket they were bowled out, in just over an hour, for just 44 runs. Lancashire, winners by 225 runs, was the only county side to inflict a defeat on the South African tourists that summer. The South Africans returned to Aigburth in 1924 and played out a drawn match with Lancashire.

1913

Mr H H Hornby, the club President and member for 65 years, passed away. The Hornby Family had been members of the Liverpool Cricket scene from its onset and the loss was keenly felt by the membership. As a mark of respect all matches were cancelled for the day.

These were distressing times at Aigburth and the country was on the brink of war. The club, to add to the sadness, was forced to announce the death of their greatest ever player, Alan Gibson Steele.

Again hospitality was shown to the visiting D'Oyly Carte Opera Company allowing them use of the nets, a privilege also afforded to one Jack Sharpe.

For whatever reason is was decided not to accept the challenge of a game from the Strolling Players but offer the game to the Football Ramblers.

The committee with clever generosity decided to lend the stands and turnstiles to the football club for their use on the condition that they maintained them and returned them in time for the summer cricketing season.

Meanwhile the same 'maintenance contract' was offered to

and accepted willingly by the Liverpool Ladies Hockey Club for the use of the old ground and Ladies Pavilion and for the first time they luxuriated in the relative comfort offered after the years spent changing before and after their winter games in cold windy tents.

Further donations were made to the club, this time in the form of two horses used in the ground maintenance where previously such livestock had been hired for the Summer season only and returned to their owners for the winter.

Records show that the Club facilities were used to host a poultry show followed by a military show, the latter, maybe not surprisingly, causing such damage to the stands that Colonel Melly was asked to contribute 50% of the repair bill.

10th July - Lancashire v Yorkshire

This was a friendly game that had been hastily arranged to coincide with a visit by King George V and Queen Mary. The Royal couple were in Liverpool to celebrate the opening of the new Gladstone Dock. The match was remembered for the record breaking bowling of Harry Dean who did in fact miss the start of the game.

Owing to overnight rain all parties agreed to a pre-arranged pitch inspection at lunchtime. Nevertheless, next morning, the sun shone brightly. So quickly did the pitch improve that the teams took to the field before the expected time. When Yorkshire began the batting Harry Dean was not at the ground. When he did eventually arrive, he produced a startling performance and helped his side to victory. Harry Dean finished the match with bowling figures of 17 for 91 as Lancashire won by 3 wickets. This is still a record haul for a Lancashire bowler in a first class match at Aigburth. The visiting side, despite their defeat, expressed their approval of the Aigburth ground. Indeed one of their number was quoted as saying *"Why this is better than Old Trafford"*. Liverpool Daily Post 11th July 1913.

1914

Danson Cunningham, a member for over 50 years, was elected as the 4th President of the Club in a year that, due to the advent of the Great War, was to see many changes. Unfortunately he was only to survive to enjoy this position for two years.

A local neighbour, a Mr. Rigsby, (obviously not a member!) complained that someone was stealing apples from his garden through a hole in the fence and whilst the Club denied any responsibility it offered to pay half of the cost of the repair.

Despite the uncertainty the Booth Holt Shipping Line hired the lower ground for the season and following war being declared the Club played the scheduled match against Bootle and then agreed that matches should continue to be played whilst awaiting developments.

10th August Lancashire v Hampshire

The nation was at war with the central powers of Europe when the match against Hampshire was played at Aigburth. A fine bowling performance, 8 for 27 by Harry Dean gave Lancashire a flying start as Hampshire struggled to a first innings total of 74 runs. John Tyldesley then produced an innings of outstanding merit. He scored 112 runs as his side ended their first innings with a lead of 152 runs. Hampshire, in reply, was all out for 125. Many of the Liverpool Cricket Club members now exchanged their whites for khaki and marched off to war.

Good use was made of the premises as the Military requisitioned the Aigburth site and a recruitment office was established with pride of place given to the notice advising the names of the brave men who volunteered.

With so many young men away at war, reluctantly most of the staff were given one month's notice to look for work elsewhere, whilst the Head Groundsman had his wages reduced to 5 shillings a week. The only other employee retained was the Barman who had replaced the recently deceased Steward.

Despite events in Europe a Mrs Barr of Beech Lane thought it important enough to complain about the colour of the bricks used in the building of the Club's perimeter wall and offered at her own expense to paint the offending stonework. Whilst permission was given the work was never undertaken.

The Aigburth Ground circa 1914

The members who were not on active service did what they could to help the war effort by staging a match, between Lancashire and Northants, in aid of the Red Cross and a temporary pistol range was sited beneath the steps of the pavilion for the use of members.

As the war progressed a second list was posted on the wall of the pavilion, sadly that of the inevitable fatalities in such a conflict, one of whom was Fredrick Turner.

Frederick Harding Turner

Frederick Turner was born at 4, Mossley Hill Drive in the Sefton Park district of Liverpool in 1888. He was educated at Greenbank and Sedburgh Schools, before being accepted to read law at Trinity College, Oxford. An excellent all round sportsmen he gained a cricket blue in 1909, while playing against the MCC at The Parks. He went on to play 5 first class cricket matches for his university. Back in his native Liverpool he opened the batting at Aigburth on many occasions but it is on the rugby field where he will be best remembered. Playing for the Liverpool club he soon earned himself the nickname of "Tanky" for his robust play. He was picked, presumably through his parentage, to play on 15 occasions for Scotland and captained them in 1914.

At the outbreak of war he was granted a commission and joined the 10th battalion (Liverpool Scottish) of the Kings Liverpool Regiment. He landed in France in November 1914. 2nd Lieutenant Frederick Turner, was shot and killed on 10th January 1915 while supervising a barbed wire arrangement near the town of Ypres. He was the first member of Liverpool Cricket Club to lose his life in the conflict. There were sadly, many more members of the club who would sacrifice their lives in defence of freedom, the most famous of whom was Noel Chavasse.

Captain Noel Godfrey Chavasse VC and Bar, MC, RAMC

Noel Chavasse was the son of Rev Francis James Chavasse and his wife Enid (nee Maude). He was born, along with his twin brother Christopher, in Oxford on the 19th November.1884. The couple had seven children in all.   In 1900 Reverend Chavasse accepted the Anglican Bishopric of Liverpool and the family moved from Oxford. They took up residence at 19 Abercromby Square, then the Bishops Palace, from where Noel and Christopher attended the Liverpool College.

Noel returned to his native Oxford in October 1904 to enter Trinity College to read natural sciences. Later that year, he was present when King Edward VII, escorted by Queen Alexandra, laid the foundation stone of the new Anglican Cathedral on St James Mount in Liverpool. The Cathedral project was close to the heart of Bishop Chavasse and is now one of the finest buildings in Britain.

The Chavasse twins excelled on the athletic track during their days at Oxford and both were awarded a "Blue", before going on to represent Great Britain on the athletic track at the 1908 Olympic Games held in London.

Noel Chavasse, during his days at Oxford, had his first taste of military life when he joined the Officers Training Corps. In 1910 he graduated from Oxford with a first class honours degree and returned to the family home in Liverpool. Noel then enrolled at Liverpool University as a full time medical student and continued an active sporting life. He ran with Sefton Harriers and became a family member of Liverpool Cricket Club. The Chavasse family were often seen "taking the air" during the warm summer weather, in the healthy environment of the Aigburth Cricket Ground.

Maybe it was the air of Aigburth that contributed to the longevity of the twin sisters of Noel, May and Marjorie, who made the Guinness Book of Records in 1988 as the oldest living twins in the world. They were then 102 years old.

The entire Chavasse Family just before the First World War

Noel was successful with his studies and, after some time spent training in Dublin, he qualified as a Doctor in 1912. He was then granted a position as a House Surgeon at the Liverpool Southern Hospital in Caryl Street.

Noel Chavasse, around this time, received his commission with the Royal Army Medical Corps and was attached to the 10th Battalion (Liverpool Scottish) of the Kings Liverpool Regiment. Following the outbreak of war the battalion arrived in France where they took heavy casualties during the fighting around the town of Hooge. As the battle raged Noel worked tirelessly under heavy fire rescuing several wounded men. He was for his efforts promoted to Captain. He was later awarded the Military Cross which he received from King George V at Buckingham Palace. Noel then returned to France.

The Liverpool Scottish next took part in the Battle of the Somme where they once again took heavy losses. The battalion made four attempts to take the heavily fortified enemy trench around the tiny village of Gullimont. Noel Chavasse, for his actions in this battle, was awarded the Victoria Cross. (A medal made from the barrel of a Russian canon that was captured at the Battle of Balaclava.)

His citation read as follows: *"On 9 August 1916, at Gullimont, France, Captain Chavasse attended to the wounded all day under heavy fire, frequently in view of the enemy, and during the night he continued searching for wounded in front of the enemy's lines. Next day, under heavy shell fire he and a stretcher bearer carried an urgent case 500 yards to safety, being wounded during the journey. The same night, with 20 volunteers, he rescued three wounded men from a shell hole 36 yards from the enemy trenches, buried the bodies of two officers and collected many identity discs. Altogether he saved the lives of some 20 wounded men."* (London Gazette 26th October 1916.)

On 5th February Noel was back at Buckingham Palace to receive his medal from the King. This much esteemed decoration was brought home to Liverpool by his cousin Marjorie. Before he returned to France, Captain Noel Chavasse was to achieve yet another objective when his offer of marriage was accepted by a young lady named Gladys whom he had long admired. Noel then left Liverpool and went back to the Western Front from where sadly, he was never to return.

The Liverpool Scottish was now to see action in the third battle of Ypres. Noel had just rejoined the battalion when he was informed of the tragic loss of his younger brother Aiden, a Lieutenant in the Kings Liverpool Regiment, who was killed in action on the 1[st]July 1917 near Hooge. His body was never found.

The soldiers of the Liverpool Scottish in the meantime had taken up position in the Weiltge sector of the Ypres salient where after going over the top, they quickly achieved their objective. Noel, along with his medical personnel, then moved forward and set up a first aid post in a captured German dugout. Noel, during the next offensive, frequently went onto the battlefield and rescued wounded men. He was hit in the back by shell splinters but refused to leave his post. Noel Chavasse, according to regimental history, was seated at a table trying to get some rest when at 3am, the position received a direct hit from a German artillery shell, He was severely wounded but managed to crawl out of the shell hole and along the trench where he was found by the men of Loyal Regiment. He was taken to No 32 casualty clearing station where, during an operation, the shell splinters were removed. The wounds, however, proved to be fatal and on 4th August 1917 Noel Chavasse died. His second citation read as follows :

"During the period 31 July to 2 August 1917, at Wieltje,

Belgium, Captain Chavasse although severely wounded early in the action while carrying a wounded officer to the dressing station, refused to leave his post and in addition to his normal duties, went out repeatedly without food, worn with fatigue and faint from his wound, he helped to carry in badly wounded men, being instrumental in saving many who would otherwise have died under the bad weather conditions. Captain Chavasse subsequently died of his wounds. (London Gazette 14th September 1917.)

Noel Chavasse is buried in the military Cemetery at Brandhoek. His headstone, erected in 1981, is the only one in the world to display two **symbols of the Victoria** Cross. He is remembered in Liverpool at several different locations.

His name is recorded at the Liverpool College while a heritage plaque may be seen on the wall of his former home at Abercromby Square. His name is inscribed on the war memorial at Liverpool Cricket Club where the front lounge is named in his honour.

The back lounge of the pavilion is also named to honour another war hero Eric Stuart Dougall V.C.,M.C.

Eric Stuart Dougall was born in Tunbridge Wells, Kent and was educated at the local school. In 1905 he entered Pembroke

College Cambridge, where he studied engineering. He proved to be an excellent sportsman and, in 1907, he was awarded a 'Blue' for representing the University on the athletics track. After graduating in 1908 he took up a position with the Mersey Docks and Harbour Board where he remained until 1912. It was during this time he was seen in the colours of Liverpool Rugby Club on the ground at Aigburth. Later, having acquired a position with the local dock company, he set sail for Bombay. At the outbreak of World War One he joined the Bombay Light Horse Regiment, and in 1915, was granted a commission with the Royal Field Artillery. He later received the Military Cross for his part in the Battle of Messines.

"For conspicuous gallantry and devotion to duty as Group Intelligence Officer and F.O.O. He took up a succession of observation posts in advanced and exposed positions, from which he successfully maintained communications with Headquarters. He was slightly wounded, but remained at duty and has frequently performed work requiring initiative under heavy fire with great coolness and gallantry". (London Gazette, August 1917.)

Eric Dougall continued to serve his country and was later awarded a Victoria Cross. His citation was as follows.... *"His majesty the King has been graciously pleased to approve of the award of a Victoria Cross to Lieutenant (Acting Captain) Eric Stuart Dougall M.C, late S.R, attd " A " Bty. , 88ᵗʰ Bde, R.F.A.*

"For most conspicuous bravery and skilful leadership in the field when in command of his battery near Messines on April 10ᵗʰ, 1918".

Captain Dougall maintained his guns in action from early morning throughout a heavy concentration of gas and high explosive shell. Finding that he could not clear the crest owing to the withdrawal of our line, Captain Dougall ran his guns to the top of the ridge to fire over open sights. By this time our infantry had been pressed back in line with the guns. Captain Dougall at once assumed command of the situation, rallied and organised the infantry, supplied them with Lewis guns and armed as many gunners as he could with rifles. With these he formed a line in front of his battery which during the period was harassing the advancing Germans with a rapid rate of fire. When one of the guns was turned over by a direct hit, and the detachment knocked out, casualties were replaced and the gun brought into action again. Although exposed to both rifle and machine gun fire, this officer fearlessly walked about as if on parade, calmly giving orders and encouraging everybody. His remark to the infantry at this juncture, "So long as you stick to your trenches, I will keep my guns here", had a most inspiring effect on all ranks. This line was maintained throughout the day, thereby delaying the enemy's advance for over twelve hours. In the evening having expended all ammunition, the battery was ordered to withdraw. This was done by manhandling the guns over a distance of about 800 yards of shell-cratered country, an almost impossible feat considering the ground and the intense machine-gun fire. Owing to Captain Dougall's personality and skilful leadership throughout this trying day, there is no doubt that a serious breach in our line was averted.

This gallant officer was unfortunately killed four days later whilst directing the fire of his battery, on Mount Kimmel."
(London Gazette, June 1918.)

Lieutenant (Acting Captain)Eric Stuart Dougall, MC, VC

During World War One as many as 170 of the members were reported to be engaged in the service of their country, all of whom were granted free membership of the club. The Liverpool area came under the control of the Western Command. The heavy casualties sustained during the conflict forced the authority to requisition many civilian buildings and convert them into temporary military hospitals. The pavilion at Aigburth was one such structure. It became a unit within the 1st Western General Hospital (Territorial Force) Liverpool which was part of the Royal Army Medical Corps. It became a hospital that contained 60 beds used for the treatment of other ranks. Cricket, as a form of convalescence, was to prove a great comfort to the wounded men and several matches, between the various Regiments, took part on the ground.

One of the more amusing 'word of mouth' tales of these times is regarding the horse that was used to pull the mower to cut the grass. As previously mentioned this was hired for the summer months and returned 'home' for the winter duration. However as all such healthy animals were requisitioned by the War Office, Miss Chintz, the owner, was having none of that and hid her horse in her bedroom for the duration of the war and only brought it out briefly when the grass was in need of trimming. It is a good tale but it could be that the Military turned a 'blind eye' because most of the regiments passing through Liverpool visited the club to play both cricket and tennis! Whatever the truth the effect was the same – Miss Chintz kept the horse and the grass got cut! Sadly at the end of the war the horse was killed in a road accident in Garston.

Despite the occupation by the military the ground continued to be used by local schools and boy scouts for sporting activities hence the complaint from Mr Rigsby that once again his orchard had been raided!

The Kings Lancashire Military Convalescent Hospital, Blackpool was one of the military sides who visited the ground and took on the Royal Army Medical Corps who was stationed at Fazackerley. Their opening batsman was Corporal Tyler who was, before the conflict, a player with Northamptonshire. He later became a professional with Liverpool Cricket Club. The

South Wales Borders also played two matches on the Aigburth ground. The first game was against an eleven drawn up from Liverpool Club players. The 88th Infantry Regiment, who was at the time billeted in the grounds of Knowsley Hall, provided the opposition in the second game. These games, along with several local matches did much to aid morale and comfort the wounded during the bitter years of conflict.

Despite all that was happening elsewhere, which was to change life forever, events still took place at Aigburth and decisions were made, some of which were immediately forgotten and some which still shape our lives today.

The club was proud to welcome Mr J.A.Brodie, the Liverpool City Surveyor, as a member of the club in 1916, a gentleman to go down in sporting history for the invention of goal nets which he patented in 1890, a year before they were first used in an F.A.Cup final.

Maybe explaining away the loss of certain memorabilia previously mentioned, the premises of Browns Buildings in the city centre were destroyed by fire, unfortunately a venue that had been chosen for the safe keeping of such artifacts!

Alas, the effects of war were beginning to be felt in this 'rich mans club'. The income reduction due to the greatly limited social use of the premises combined with the expense of the ground maintenance plunged the club into the red once again and the sum of £700 was needed to balance the books. An appeal was made under the slogan 'Let's get the club out of debt before our boys come home' and such was the wealth of the 'rich men' that the debt was immediately reduced to just £100.

Slowly the nation, along with her allies, began to overwhelm the Central Powers of Europe and in November 1918 an armistice was declared. It had been a long and bitter conflict with victory being won with a heavy cost in human life. The

Military slowly began to leave Aigburth and some semblance of the old order began to reassert itself at Liverpool Cricket Club.

1919

A meeting was convened in the Spring of 1919 in the pavilion at Aigburth that was attended by the secretaries of all the senior cricket clubs on Merseyside. It was agreed, by all concerned, to start the season with just one team from each club with second elevens being formed as the men were de-mobbed. Mr. E Roper informed the membership that he would shortly, after many years of service, be stepping down from his duties as club secretary. He was promptly rewarded with a life membership. Joseph Bruce Ismay, who was moving to London, announced his resignation from the club.

J. BRUCE ISMAY

OWNER OF THE TITANIC

MEMBER OF CLUB UNTIL 1919

Joseph Bruce Ismay

Joseph Bruce Ismay was born in Waterloo, Crosby on 12th December 1862. He was the eldest of the three boys born to Thomas Ismay, the owner of the White Star shipping line. After Harrow, Bruce Ismay was sent to France to complete his education before taking up a position with the White Star Line. Following a lengthy apprenticeship he was sent to New York where he became the agent for the Company.

On the 4th December 1888 he married Francis Shieffelin before returning to Liverpool aboard RMS Adriatic. The couple lived at the home of the Ismay family, a house named 'Dawpool', at Thurstaston before they purchased a home of their own in Mossley Hill. The house, now demolished, was called 'Sandheys'. Bruce Ismay became a member of Liverpool Cricket Club and represented them both at the crease and on the tennis court. He also played soccer with Liverpool Ramblers. The Ismay brothers, thanks to their considerable wealth, later established a cricket team at the family home at 'Dawpool.' where they numbered, amongst their fixtures, a game with an XI from Liverpool.

In 1899, following the death of his father, Bruce Ismay became president of the White Star shipping line. In 1912 he set sail aboard the RMS Titanic from Southampton on her maiden voyage to New York. On Sunday April 14, the most famous night in British Maritime history, the liner struck an iceberg and sank with the loss of 1,523 lives. Bruce Ismay was amongst the 705 people who survived. He later faced an inquiry in both New York and London and was exonerated of any blame for the sinking. Bruce Ismay, his career now ruined, later sold the family home at Mossley Hill and moved to the Mayfair district of London. He suffered from ill health in the later years of his life and died on 17th October 1937. He was 74.

1919

With the end of the war the club applied to the Military to reoccupy the premises and then needed to try to restore it to its former glory. Once again the begging bowl went out to the members who were able to raise £800 for the refurbishment.

As evidence of the inflation that had taken hold the lower ground was once again hired out, this time to The Holt Shipping Line, for an annual rent of £150, an increase of 650% in just 8 years.

As some recompense for the items lost in the fire, the owners of Browns Building presented portraits of the President Charles Hannay and Teddy Roper the Secretary, to the club, both of which are still to be found adorning the walls of the committee room.

Normality was slowly returning to the sporting activities and whilst the Cheshire County Cricket Club were allowed to use the ground for part of the season, the Rugby Club started playing again as did the Ladies Hockey team. A forward looking committee voted to replace the four footed horse power with a motor mower, therefore dispensing with the necessity of keeping an animal.

1920

Although times were changing and a proposition put to the AGM that the club should open on a Sunday at 2pm. met some opposition, the motion was carried on the understanding that no intoxicating liquor would be sold. Tea only would be available.

3rd July - Lancashire v Hampshire

This match, the first on the ground for nearly six years, produced a most exciting finish. The start of play was delayed due to the heavy rain, so thousands of people gathered outside the enclosure awaiting the umpire's decision. The crowds, as start of play was announced, rushed the main gate invading the ground, enclosure and pavilion. It was estimated, in the confusion that followed, that about 3,000 people gained free admission. There was a large cheer when Harry Makepeace, accompanied by Charlie Hallows, appeared on the pavilion steps and the period of inter-war cricket got underway at Aigburth.

Lancashire, thanks to a top score of 65 by Makepeace, started their second innings with a lead of 8 runs over their opponents. They were then dismissed for 57 runs leaving Hampshire to score just 66 runs to win. The pitch however gave the visitors no help at all. Their last 5 wickets were lost for just 10 runs as the home side, much to the delight of the crowd, won the game by a single run.

1921

The committee announced the death of Edward Roper who had died following an operation to remove his appendix.

The loss of this popular person was felt throughout the sporting circles of the Liverpool area. Edward Roper had dedicated his life to cricket during the summer months, and had proved a tireless exponent in the execution of his duties both on and off the field. The son of a wealthy banker, 'Teddy' Roper was born in Richmond, Yorkshire in 1851 and educated at Clifton Public School. Around 1875, after settling in Liverpool, he became closely involved with Sefton Cricket Club before making his debut for Lancashire against Derbyshire in 1874. One year later he made his debut for his native Yorkshire against Middlesex at Lords. He played many a fine innings at Sefton before, in 1893, he transferred his allegiance to the Liverpool Club at Aigburth. He made his last first class appearance, in 1893, when he opened the innings for the Liverpool & District XI against Yorkshire at Aigburth. He played with the Liverpool Racquets Club and took part in the annual quoits match between Liverpool and Childwall. He was reported to have had a mellifluous singing voice that could be admired without musical accompaniment. He was, along with certain other members, often to be seen at Aigburth during the war years where his enthusiastic manner and cheerful countenance helped many a 'Tommy' on his road to full recovery. Edward Roper was, at the time of his death, residing in the Mossley Hill area of Liverpool.

A fitting memorial to 'Teddy' was called for from clubs across Merseyside and after the usual suggestions of plaques, cups or similar trophies two small score boxes painted black, were erected in his name with a suitable plaque on each, one of which has withstood the ravages of time and over 80 years later is still in use.

1922

The rugby players suggested that a plaque be placed in the pavilion in remembrance of those members who had lost their lives during the Great War. A London firm was commissioned to carry out this task and they completed the job in 1922. On 30th April it was unveiled in the pavilion. The local press covered the event and published the following report. ... *The members of Liverpool Cricket and Rugby Football Clubs yesterday afternoon paid tribute to the memory of their comrades who fell in the war, when Colonel J V Campbell V.C. unveiled a memorial tablet of oak with the names of seventy one members inscribed, in the pavilion of the cricket club at Aigburth. There was a large gathering, and the proceedings were of an impressive character.*

Canon Ainslie said that they were met on a very solemn, though not necessarily a sorrowful occasion, for they looked more with pride than with sorrow upon the losses they had sustained during the terrible war. They in Liverpool must feel justly proud of those sons who had stood up for their country when the crisis came. He hoped it was the last war to be fought, for the world was for peaceful men. It was passion and greed that caused wars, and they must get those passions out of their minds before nations could live at peace with one another. Colonel Campbell, after unveiling the memorial, said that their lads had gone out to fight with a firm and calm determination to win. They had something that was learned on those playing grounds, and which the people they were fighting against did not understand - that of playing a losing game. There were times when it looked like being a losing game, for things were bad. A club like theirs had done its bit for England, for it taught its men how to play a losing game, to meet the odds with a firm determination to win, and that took a great deal of learning. Those men had gone and set an example of courage and manhood which they must follow if they were to pull England through.

At the conclusion of the service, Mr. Archie Tod, one of the vice-presidents of the club, thanked Colonel Campbell on behalf of the members for unveiling the memorial and also for his address.

Liverpool City Council, later that year, informed the committee of their forthcoming plans for the development of the Aigburth district. They requested that the Club relinquish a 60 foot wide strip of land in order to widen the road. It was decided, after a lengthy discussion, that a 16 foot strip, at 4 shillings a square foot, be surrendered on condition that the main gate (not evident today) be removed from the centre of the wall and the Riversdale Road gate, moved back. The Club also requested that the buildings that had to be demolished were rebuilt elsewhere at the expense of the council. The Club, following these alterations, built stables on the former site of the main gate, added an extension to the lodge, and moved the garden and bicycle sheds to another part of the site. The ground was now beginning to take on a formation we recognise to-day.

1923

The club finances were now showing a handsome profit and several improvements were made to the Aigburth ground. A new toilet block, complete with penny slot machines, was built along Riversdale Road and perimeter railings removed and replaced with a high brick wall. New wicket covers were bought and the location fitted with a set of sight screens, at an extra £28, which were painted green. The railway embankment, due to the bad winter that followed, collapsed and the cost of the repairs, after much dispute, was met by the Cheshire Lines Committee.

Only three years on from the agreement to open the Club on a Sunday complaints were received that tennis was being played as early as 9 o'clock on a Sunday morning and it was left to the Steward to remind members that this was not allowed until after 2pm.

1924

Mr A.L.Melly was elected President.

Mr Visasto a member and collector of cricket memorabilia donated a copy of "The Cricket Boy", the original of which is to be found adorning the wall at Lords. This still hangs at the entrance to the lounge today. Also donated was a copy of the first match report from 1881 which unfortunately is no longer to be found on the club premises, but this is one loss that cannot be put down to the fire at Browns Buildings. Maybe one day it may be returned.

14th May - Lancashire v Glamorgan

The start of this match was delayed by rain. Lancashire, despite a first innings total of 49 runs, still managed to beat the Welsh side that were appearing at Aigburth for the first time. The visitors in reply produced the lowest score ever seen in a first class match on the Liverpool ground. They were all out for 22 runs. It is still today the lowest score made in a first class innings against Lancashire. The home side went on to win by 107 runs.

1925

One gentleman was kind enough to donate 17 copies of Wisden's Annuals to the club, but unfortunately they are no longer in the Club's possession and once again the committee felt that it would be fitting to display portraits of all the Presidents.

As long ago as 1904 Mr A.L.Melly had been asked to locate the history of the Club including paintings of Past Presidents and the Club minutes. He was unsuccessful possibly due to the nomadic years before the Club had their own pavilion.

4th July Lancashire v Sussex

The attendance record at Aigburth was set on this day. Sharp and Makepeace were included in the Lancashire line up but the main attraction was the appearance in the Sussex team of Maurice Tate. The burly England all-rounder was at the height of his fame having just returned from the MCC tour of Australia. His popularity drew a crowd of 11,000 to Aigburth, 9,200 of whom paid for admission at the gate. A fine knock by Charlie Hallows, 163, was the highlight of the match that followed; Lancashire went on to win by an innings and 144 runs.

1926

These were exhilarating days at Aigburth and money was in plentiful supply. Extensive repairs were carried out to the pavilion and stands, while new turnstiles were fitted at the main gates. The tennis section continued to be very successful and popular with the members. Cricket, due to a lack of interest, was confined to the top field while the lower ground was rented out to various local companies. This arrangement helped to swell the coffers of the Club. The main pitch however was still proving a headache.

Samples of turf and soil were sent away for analysis. The problem, when the results were known, appeared to be caused by the lack of drainage. The lower field was also giving trouble.

Mr. Sutton of Sutton's Seeds was asked for his advice and he suggested potatoes should be planted. This was not done. Part of the lower ground was ploughed up, rolled, and made into a turf nursery. This sale of turf over the years caused the level of the field to drop by several feet as can still be seen today on close inspection.

1927

A team from the Gold Coast touring Lancashire asked for the privilege to play at Liverpool and whilst this met with agreement no details are to be found as to whether this went ahead and if so with what result.

A request from LCC to the Cheshire Lines Railway Company also met with agreement. This was for permission for members to have access to the railway line to retrieve any cricket or tennis balls sent over the railings with a wayward shot. Almost unbelievably this was granted at a cost of two shillings and sixpence with no liability to attach to the Railway Company. Whether this payment was an annual fee or a one off payment is not recorded but it certainly does not pertain today.

A spot check on the bar accounts revealed a deficit of 31 bottles of gin and 1600 pints of beer. When asked to account for it the steward had no answer so was dismissed. Owing to his wife being sick he was allowed to stay but unpaid. The steward had an unblemished record so further checks were made; it would seem that members paid for their drinks at the end of the week. Their drinks were put on a chalk slate behind the bar and then were being rubbed off when nobody was looking. So much for honour amongst gentlemen!

The steward was reinstated and told to keep an eye on the members and a new till was installed.

1928

By now the Club had a considerable library as evidenced by the necessity to purchase another bookcase and further Wisden's were given by Mr Visasto who had donated many books over the years. Mr Patterson was also kind enough to donate a

Barograph for use, and whilst this stood for many years on the bar as recently as to be in living memory, its present whereabouts are unknown. However there is no record of it ever being sold.

1929

26th June, Lancashire v Leicestershire

The visitors won the toss and elected to bat. A fine display of batting by England star George Geary (102) helped them to score 292 runs in their first innings. Jack Iddon then hit himself into the record books. This right hander scored the highest total yet seen by a Lancashire player on the Aigburth ground. With his score standing at 222, he was finally bowled by Alf Coleman as Lancashire reached a total of 502 runs. The match ended in a draw.

It was around this time that due to its many changes the pavilion began to take on the shape that is recognised to-day. The ground floor now consisted of a large changing room and large kitchen. There were also store rooms and a wine cellar plus living accommodation for the Steward and his family. As the call for more meals increased the bar space was reduced, forcing the committee to add yet more rooms to the building. A kitchen and bedrooms were built on the side of the club for the Steward and family   A small set of stairs for staff use only linked the kitchens with the large members changing facilities on the upper floor.

The staff, in 1929 was listed as follows: The steward, his wife, who acted as the cook, with two kitchen staff, two waitresses, one barman and a scullery maid. There was also a male changing room attendant. Some of these during the Summer months occupied the rooms above the stables but when the cricket season ended they would be relieved of their posts and the building closed down. The rugby players, during the Winter months used only the changing rooms on the ground floor which provided very limited washing facilities.

1930

14th May Lancashire v Australia

Nine times an Australian touring team visited Aigburth, the most notable of which, is mentioned above. The great Donald George Bradman made his only first class appearance on the Liverpool ground. His presence attracted a 1st day crowd of over 5,000. Lancashire, who batted first, struggled against the bowling of Grimmett and Hornibrook. Only Peter Eckersley passed the 50 mark and they were all out for 176 runs. Bradman batting number 3 was bowled by his fellow countryman Ted MacDonald for 9 runs as the tourists ended the day on 63 for 5.

There was a slow build up of spectators the next day. Rain delayed the start so an early lunch was taken. When play commenced, the Australians were all out for 115 which was, to date, their lowest score of the tour. Lancashire ended the day on 101 for 5. Some late resistance from Eckersley (38) on the final day, left Australia needing 226 to win. Bradman, when he arrived at the wicket, chose to bat with caution and the match ended in a draw. There were ironic cheers from the crowd when late in the match the "Don" at last drove Eckersley to the boundary. Australia, after batting for 60 overs, ended on 137 for 2. The fixture, over the three day period, was watched by over 16,000 people.

1931

A year of celebration! The club was to recognise 50 years of occupation of their Aigburth premises starting with a Grand Ball at the Adelphi Hotel and throughout the summer season enjoyed various events. A quoits match took place after which a tennis exhibition was held. But the highlight of the festivities must have been the cricket match not played to MCC rules. The conditions of play between the male and female teams stipulated that all the men had to dress as W G Grace and bat with broom handles! The outcome of the encounter went unrecorded.

To add to the enjoyment of the spectators the L.M.S. Brass Band played throughout the afternoon and cocktails were available at 1 shilling each.

11ᵗʰ July Lancashire v New Zealand

The New Zealanders on their first tour of England won the toss and chose to open the batting. The Kiwis then promptly hit their way into the record book. They kept Lancashire in field all day and, at the close had reached 410 for the loss of 9 wickets. This was the first time a touring team had scored over 400 runs in one day at Aigburth. Next day it was the turn of the home side. The Kiwi bowlers toiled on a lifeless pitch as Lancashire finished the day on 487 for 7. The final day saw the New Zealanders score over 300 runs as the match ended in a draw.

The club still having no use for the lower ground continued to hire it out to the Rugby Club in the Winter and St Christopher's School in the Summer.

Visiting teams could only have tea if they supplied the same to the Liverpool Club on the return fixture. They could however have high tea for the sum of 1/6 pence if they booked a few days in advance. Lunch at Liverpool was considered a rare privilege.

1932

Among the cricketing fixtures this year was one between a visiting team from South America and a District team and whilst the result is not important history was made as for the first time a visiting team was allowed the use of the upstairs changing facilities. Although at a later committee meeting it was decided that this hospitality would generally not be afforded to visiting teams.

Catering in the pavilion continued to be provided by the Steward and his wife whilst any refreshment arrangement outside went out to tender. This was usually won by The Liverpool City Caterers for a flat payment of £25 plus 7.5% of the profits.

11th June Lancashire v India

The team representing the Indian sub-continent looked in at Aigburth during their first ever tour of England. The game was in preparation for their inaugural Test match that was due to be played at Lords in two weeks time. The Tourists, captained by N G Navle, won the toss, and elected to bat. They soon won over the crowd with their delicate style of play as centuries by both Nayudu and L Amar Singh saw them through to a first innings total of 493. Lancashire, at the end of day two, had reached 232/2, this mainly thanks to an unbeaten century by Eddie Paynter. The home side, when play recommenced, batted on to make 399. India, in reply, were on 36/2, when the game was abandoned as a draw. The Indian touring side appeared again at Aigburth in 1936.

24th August Lancashire v Gloucestershire

This match was dominated by the powerful presence of Wally Hammond and the England star treated the Aigburth crowd to an admirable display of batting. He made a cautious start and ended the day, after batting for four hours on 129. Next day he went on to reach 264 before being caught off the bowling of Butterworth. This is still the highest score achieved, in a first class match, by a batsman on the Aigburth ground. Lancashire then, in their first innings, made 248 and accepted the "follow on ". The match, with the home side batting out time, ended in a draw.

Playing in this match was Edwin Alan Barlow MBE (1912 – 1980) one of Liverpool Cricket Club's most outstanding athletes; educated at Kingsland Grange, Shrewsbury and Oxford University he excelled at many sports and captained his school at cricket and soccer. In his first game for Oxford University against Minor Counties he took eight wickets which included two hat tricks in the same innings. After leaving university he played for Lancashire at both cricket and tennis in the same year. He also played soccer for Manchester United and as a squash player represented the North of England whilst being recognised as one of the top four of all England.

The attendances, which remained on the decline, compelled the club committee to look at alternative ways of generating income. It was decided the lower field was to be hired out to a local school, while the Rugby section had its rent increased to £110 per annum.

Mr. Bernard Tyler, who was a professional bowler on the grounds staff, took up the vacant position and his family would from then on form a lasting relationship with Liverpool Cricket Club.

Decisions for the committee this year included a complaint about the playing of "Yo Yos' in the club on which they declined to comment and agreeing (again) to obtain pictures of all the Past Presidents to hang in the committee room, which was finally achieved in 2006.

1933

1st July Lancashire v West Indies

The West Indian side brought semi-tropical weather with them when they arrived at Liverpool. This brought an inquisitive crowd of over 6, 000 people to witness this historical occasion. The visitors had been granted test status in 1928 and, one week previous, had lost by an innings in their first ever test match against England at Lords.

The touring side won the toss and, on an excellent wicket, decided to bat. Their innings lasted until late in the day when they were all out for a total of 305 runs. Lancashire, at the close, was 7 for no wicket. Next morning the home side began strongly. Len Hopwood and Cyril Washbrook put on an opening stand of 169 before Washbrook was out with his score on 95. Hopwood went on to make a total of 112 as Lancashire ended the day at 351 for 5. Lancashire, on the final day, finished their first innings with a lead of 88 runs. West Indies then made 240 for 5 before the match was abandoned as a draw.

In 1939 The West Indies, visited Aigburth for a second time.

Commercialisation was beginning to emerge into the everyday aspect of the Liverpool Cricket Club when Mr Jack Sharpe was asked to sell cricket bats and tennis rackets on the site and the first purpose built refreshment hut was built on the Riverside Road side of the ground. Whether this was to increase the club's revenue figures or just to add to the benefits for the members is open to speculation.

1934

For the first time gentlemen were allowed to use the Ladies Pavilion. But for what?

1935

Maybe all this activity proved too much for the groundsman Mr. Meads who, after many years of faithful service, decided the time was right to retire. He had been with the club since 1920 and had not in all those years, been granted one penny of increase to his pay. The club committee, in deference to his many years of service, presented him with a cheque for £50.

Application was made for shops to be built on the estate of the late Mr Brodie in Aigburth Road, opposite the Club's ground. The committee decided to stand firm with the neighbours and together their objections were strong enough to have the plans rejected.

1936

All the crickets clubs on Merseyside held a meeting at the Club and together decided to adopt the new LBW rule for the coming season.

1937

The top ground was reported to be infested with a weed called Yarrow and an expert was brought in to cure it. In the Summer months whilst the bottom ground, still not being used by LCC and the contract with St Christopher's having expired, was offered to the City Council with the Rugby Club still renting the pitch for the Winter.

Members wishing to extend the available sport facilities further, asked about the possibility of having a Badminton court built on the perimeter of the ground. Whilst this was considered enquiries made to local Badminton Clubs resulted in no further action being taken in this respect. Plans for a swimming pool were also considered and then vetoed.

The Ladies Hockey Association played an International match at Aigburth between England and Ireland.

1938

One of the better if not the best decision taken this year was the employment of the groundsman's son Ray Tyler as a net bowler for 15 shillings a week.

The county match between Lancashire and Derby was broadcast on the 'wireless' for the first time.

1939

Storm clouds hanging over Europe broke prematurely when on 14 June 1939, Lancashire and Sussex attempted to play off their county fixture at Aigburth. The match had to be abandoned without a ball being bowled owing to the persistent rain. The outcome was disappointing for the local cricket fans that would now not see county cricket played again at Aigburth for another seven years. On 3rd September, Britain declared war on Germany.

The premises at Aigburth then began slowly to shutdown. The remaining stocks of wines and spirits were sold off to members before the pavilion was requisitioned by the military. The R A F, who were first to arrive, swiftly anchored a large barrage balloon on the top ground while the Royal Navy occupied the lower field. Many of the members were called to the services whilst those who remained at home did as much as possible to help the war effort. The A.R.P. took over the top changing room. The R.A.F. left the ground after twelve months to be replaced by units of the Home Guard. An inventory was made of the furniture before it was put into storage while apparatus for fighting fires was placed around the club. These devices were deemed necessary as for the first time in history Liverpool was attacked from the air.

The German Air Force (The Luftwaffe) attacked Merseyside on numerous occasions between August 1940 and January 1942. On 19th August, Walton Jail was hit resulting in the loss of 22 lives. On 28th November 164 people were killed when a bomb hit a shelter under a school on Durning Road in the Edge Hill district of Liverpool. (This is thought to be the biggest loss of life caused by a single bomb dropped on Britain.)

The raids continued over Christmas and on into 1941 when Liverpool suffered eight nights of continuous bombing. This period will be forever remembered as the 'May Blitz'. Germany prior to its planned invasion of Russia made one last attempt to obliterate the port of Liverpool. Between the dates of 1st to 7th of May 1941, they dropped 112,000 incendiaries and 870 tonnes of high explosive bombs on Merseyside killing over 1,500 people and making over 50,000 homeless. The docks however, continued to function and import the much needed aid from America who was, later that year, to enter the war on the side of Britain.

One of the Luftwaffe pilots (maybe having an active dislike of cricket) saved one bomb for the cricket club. He missed the club but scored a direct hit on the bridge between the two grounds which was totally destroyed. The club had the roof of the canteen blown off and the windows on the front of the club blown in. As the club was designated for military use the bridge was repaired immediately but the club had to wait for the war to end to replace its roof and windows.

It was now the turn of Germany to suffer massive bombing raids before her final annihilation. In May 1945, the war was over and the Allies were victorious.

During the years 1939 to 1945 the committee had continued to meet, although not on a regular basis, and records tell of their request to members to continue to use the somewhat limited facilities available to them in order to help the finances of the Club. To also help the bank balance or maybe the morale of the members (or both), the bar started to open on Sunday evenings from 6 to 9 o'clock.

Maybe to help the morale of the navel command in Scotland, Liverpool Cricket Club sent them ten pairs of quoits. Whether they were ever used for their intended purpose or melted down for the war effort, who knows.

Benefits derived from the occupation by the military included no taxes or rates payable and unlike all their domestic neighbours they did not lose their metal railings to the war effort.

Such cricket matches that were arranged at other venues saw members having to carry their own bags for the first time due to the shortage of petrol, the Club's allowance being only 18 gallons per month.

Further restrictions from the Ministry of Food denied sporting clubs a food permit as they were not considered catering establishments, after which all provision of refreshments ceased and as a result meetings of the committee became even less frequent and the affairs of the Club were vested in the President and the Treasurer.

Aigburth cricket ground had, in the face of adversity, done its utmost to endure the six years of hardship caused by the war. The location had remained open throughout the conflict and several games of cricket between sides from the military took place on the top ground. The years of neglect had, alas, taken its toll on the premises and left them in need of refurbishment. Getting permission to do the repair work was to prove difficult as certain restrictions, with regards to building materials, were still in place. The committee, in order to carry out any repairs, would need a licence from the Ministry of Works. The groundsman was told it would take 18 months to have a new cooker installed while even new cricket equipment required a licence. Eventually, as the restrictions were lifted, a semblance of normality returned to the Aigburth enclosure and local cricket matches recommenced.

CHAPTER 4

To the Millennium

1946

At the end of hostilities the local cricket teams were quick to re-establish the club matches that had for many years provided them with regular fixtures. The local newspapers, to acknowledge these games, published a weekly table they called 'The Liverpool Competition'. First appearing in 1892 it re-appeared at the end of the war.

The crease at Aigburth, in the years immediately following the conflict, was occupied by one of the most talented cricketers that Liverpool has ever produced, Kenneth Cranston.

Ken Cranston

Born in Aigburth in 1917, Ken Cranston has the unusual distinction of captaining Lancashire on his first appearance in a first class cricket match. He began his playing days as a junior with the Liverpool Club before moving to Neston Cricket club and making his Lancashire debut against Oxford University at the Parks in May 1947. In June that year, before a packed crowd, he captained Lancashire against Glamorgan at Aigburth. His all round ability was quickly noticed by the England selectors and in July he made his test match debut against South Africa at Old Trafford. He again represented England in the remaining two matches of the series before being selected to tour the West Indies during the winter that followed.

He was appointed as Vice Captain under G.O.Allan who sustained an injury on the voyage to Barbados and missed the first two test matches. Ken Cranston was left to captain the England side in the first test at Bridgetown, Barbados. He was, due to the continued absence of G O Allan, to captain the side in the second test at the Queens Park Oval in Trinidad. Both matches ended in a draw. The series was won eventually by the home side. The team was plagued by injuries and Ken Cranston lost favour with the selectors. He played only one more test match, against Australia, the following Summer. In 1948, due to the commitments of his dental practice, he resigned the captaincy of Lancashire and, apart from one or two festival matches, retired from first class cricket. In 1993 Ken Cranston was the President of Lancashire Cricket Club and continued to practice dentistry until his retirement.

Sadly Ken Cranston died during the writing of this history on 10th January 2007.

Modernisation was to reach the club house with the installation of a hot water system which provided a warm welcome to the returning men, including those of the Rugby Club who announced their intention to re-form for the following year and needed permission to play on the ground once again.

The Ladies Hockey also returned to the club but not to enjoy the luxury of hot water as they were still changing in the Ladies Pavilion.

Once again the Club appealed to the members to donate what they could to fund the refurbishment necessary and the sum of £750 was raised. To put this amount of money in context the bar prices at this time were as follows:

Whisky 1/ 9d (8.75 pence in decimal currency)
Gin 1/ 9d (8.75 pence in decimal currency)
Sherry 2/- (10 pence in decimal currency)
Port 2 /- (10 pence in decimal currency)
Beer 7d (2.9 pence in decimal currency)

To accompany refreshments purchased at these prices a catering licence was granted to the club and meals were once again to be served from the beginning of the (cricket) season.

It was recommended that wooden bars be put over the windows, not for security reasons, but post war building materials being so poor the glass was so thin it presented a safety hazard.

1947

It must have been with considerable reluctance that agreement was reached to allow the Rugby Club to use the top ground as requested, as the conditions stated that:

1. Matches could only be played from 1st November to the 2nd Saturday in February.
2. The decision to play be taken by the groundsman who shall have full power to stop a game at any time.
3. A member of staff should attend all matches to retrieve all balls and no other person be allowed on the cricket square or tennis courts.

Further, as they now had more than one team, they were to keep looking for an additional ground.

Should it become necessary for one of the two hockey clubs now using the ground to be given notice it was to be Sefton Hockey Club with Liverpool Ladies allowed to use the pitch in front of the pavilion.

Maybe the welcome was not as warm as the water!

1948

Was the welcome any warmer for the ladies who were at last allowed to use the main lounge, the Red Room, on 'special occasions'. Maybe they took advantage of this major innovation to refresh themselves after the Tennis Exhibition arranged by the tennis section.

1949

The groundman's report on the state of the ground necessitated the Ladies Hockey club being advised that they were not being offered the use of the pitch this year or for the foreseeable future. No mention is made of the Rugby Club other than to note that they intended to introduce a new sport to the site. Basketball was to be played on the driveway at the side of the cricket pitch. No further mention is ever made of this sport so whether it ever happened or not is open for debate - unless someone can remember and fill in the missing details.

After the success of the dance held at the Drill Hall in Aigburth it was decided that this should become an annual event, though who attended is not clear, but as the Ladies Hockey were once again told they could not use the ground because of the poor state of the pitch presumably they were not there. By this time there were sufficient numbers of gentlemen members to ensure that when Lancashire played at Aigburth all the stewards were local men.

The men who unfortunately did not return after the war were remembered on the memorial originally displayed after World War One – 'the war to end all wars'.

Lancashire v New Zealand at Aigburth in 1949

1950

Despite the all male committee realising that including the 'Lady Subscribers' there was sufficient potential business to justify opening 7 days a week, in reality this was not to happen for another 6 years. Membership was healthy, so much so that too much use of the grass tennis courts resulted for the first time in the history of the club in the restriction of any further Lady Subscribers.

Funds were now available for an ongoing refurbishment of the buildings and ground and a water sprinkler was ordered together with new grass cutters and rollers. Major repairs were done to the Ladies Pavilion whilst gas fires were installed to add to the comfort of the men in the upstairs changing room.

Lancashire agreed to contribute to the building of new men's toilets on both sides of the ground and the BBC paid 15 guineas (£15.75p) to broadcast the West Indies match.

1951

Slowly in the aftermath of the war the population of Liverpool, and therefore the membership of the Club, was changing, with the wealthy merchants moving South leaving the running of their companies in the control of business men who were not in a position to play cricket during the week. Most matches were now played at the weekends other than those between companies who hired out the pitch for the day.

Professional bowlers ceased to be employed to bowl at the nets for the enjoyment/training of the members and as the Club still had no reason to use the bottom ground for its own activities this was rented out to the Gas Company.

1952

When the Liverpool League was standardised in 1949 the Club had been quick to make its mark. Under the captaincy of A E Husband Liverpool Cricket Club 1st XI were champions in both 1952 and 1953 and joint winners in 1954. In this three year period they lost only four games and according to some of the members this was the finest team the Club had fielded since the war. It was not until 1959 that they were able to celebrate 'championship status' again, this time under the captaincy of Ray Tyler.

Ray Tyler

No account of Liverpool Cricket Club would be complete without recording the huge input of the son of one of the club's early head groundsmen, Bernard Tyler. Ray Tyler was born at Wisbech Hospital in the county of Norfolk on October 26th 1922. Some time later, with his parents and sister Janet, he moved to his father's birthplace at Ridlington in the tiny county of Rutland. Ray began playing cricket while attending school at Uppingham and later joined the cricket club at the county town of Oakham. Here he played alongside both his father and his grandfather Ralph.

In 1935, following the retirement of Jack Meads, Ray's father Bernard had accepted the job of head groundsman at Liverpool and, along with his family, moved into the Lodge Cottage at Aigburth. Ray attended Gilmour School and at 15 he began an engineering apprenticeship with Liverpool Corporation Transport Department in their maintenance depot on Edge Lane. In 1930 he began playing cricket for Sefton where he remained until volunteering for military service in 1942. Ray, with his engineering skills, was posted to the Royal Navy depot at Portsmouth before being transferred to India where he remained until the end of the war.

After being demobbed, he joined Liverpool Cricket Club and played for the Liverpool first XI until the 1970s scoring over 12,000 runs, including 12 centuries, and taking 737 wickets. In 1958 he became the first batsman to score over a 1,000 runs in the Liverpool Competition and, in 1959, was elected first team captain. Liverpool Cricket Club, under his captaincy, set a record. On their way to the championship they beat all the other 15 league members in consecutive matches.

Ray Tyler, later in his career, continued to play his cricket for Liverpool, captaining both the Sunday and the second XIs. He then went on to play for the 3rd and 4th XIs until his retirement from the game in 1993. He had played competitive cricket in six decades.

In 1948 he married local girl Gwen Hughes who provided him with two sons, Christopher and Phillip. Gwen, over the years, was Ray's most devoted fan and until her death in 2001 was to prove his greatest supporter. Ray Tyler, now in his 80s, is still to be seen, on a regular basis, at Aigburth. He continues to enjoy his cricket which he now shares with his three grandchildren, whilst taking an active interest in the local cricket society.

A special function was held on Sunday 27th October 2002 to celebrate his 80th Birthday and honour one of Liverpool Cricket Club's most longstanding servants. The occasion was enjoyed by all who attended, and was a fitting tribute to many years of loyal service given to the Club by the Tyler Family.

1954

Halcyon days for the Club. Membership was steadily increasing and the cricket teams were winning most of their matches. The Rugby Club wished to have the small tubs replaced with one large communal bath within the pavilion, a request that was granted on the condition that the Rugby Club maintained it and paid for the heating of the water through a separate meter.

1956

Control of the Club by the General Committee was challenged when a question was asked at the AGM as to whether house members could have a say in the running of the club by being included in the voting procedures. Not wishing to lose overall control this was denied but agreement was given for the formation of a House Committee with one of the members allowed to attend the General Committee meetings. Needless to say women, still only Lady Subscribers, although at 295 they outnumbered the full playing members (170) and the house members (275), were not even considered in this innovation. Juniors at the time numbered 125.

The value of House Members was beginning to be realized and in order to attract new members refurbishment of the bar area was necessary and a brewery was approached for a loan to refit both the bar and the Red Room. The brewery agreed £1,350 was not sufficient for the planned renovations and a further loan from a bank was sought. Although this was available the rate of interest to be charged was too high to be acceptable. The benevolence of the President Mr T.B.Tod was such that he came to the rescue and agreed to lend the club the necessary funds free of charge for five years, set amounts to be paid back until the debt was repaid. This generous offer was gladly accepted and once again an appeal for money was made to the members.

1957

Unfortunately this time the appeal was not successful and the club could not afford to meet it debts when only £350 was raised. Adding to the problem was the new rating system introduced by the Liverpool City Council which saw an increase in this annual expenditure from £350 to £700. Although the amount of the increase was 100% an appeal was to no avail.

Passing on some of the effects of this inflation the rent to the Rugby Club for the bottom ground was increased to £160.

Extra revenue was still needed and at last the decision taken in 1950 to open the club all year round was put into effect. New indoor activities were sought and a table tennis table was purchased for use during the week. Various money spinning events were considered but the biggest change of all was that the Rugby Club were made Honorary Members for the Winter season, to help swell the bar profits.

It must be remembered that up to this time the club closed at the end of September until the end of April except for Saturdays when the Rugby needed use of the baths.

Sadly for the heritage of this great club the financial position was such that some of the silverware had to be forfeited and the cups presented by Mr A.L.Melly and Mr A.G.Steele together with the School Tour Cigar Box were sold for a total of just £58. Whether they were melted down for the value of the metal or whether any of them still exist today is unknown.

In these desperate times a light did shine on the horizon as Ladies were now sanctioned to use the Red Room after 7pm but only when there were no functions. Should they have the temerity to arrive early they had to wait outside, causing several disputes between the members.

1958

Considerable damage was caused to the club premises in March of this year by the Rugby Club, maybe celebrating their season's successes or just bewailing the end of another sporting year. Honorary Members or not they were charged for the repairs.

The recently constructed housing estate at the end of Beechwood Road, due to the increased use, had caused potholes in the surface of the thoroughfare and whilst the City Council adopted this road they asked the Club to pay a large amount towards the repairs. Stating that they had no use for this road as permission had been refused for an entrance to the lower ground they refused to make any contribution, but the argument was not over.

Argument also developed between the Club and the Rugby Club as to the correct level of rent for the bottom ground. The figure requested was £400, a sum said to be unaffordable to the Rugby Club, but after being advised that a realistic rent would be more in the region of £500, agreement was finally reached at £350 as part of a five year contract restricting further increases in that period to no more than £20 a year.

1959

At the end of the AGM a hot-pot supper was held after which members enjoyed the words of the guest speaker Cyril Washbrook - a forerunner of the Sporting Evenings still held today.

The second payment on the loan was made from the profits of the 'football pool' resumed the previous year, together with proceeds from the Kramer Tennis Circuit Tournament.

No details are available as to what form the 'football pool' took, but no evidence of a Gaming or Lottery licence can be found so presumably this in no way threatened Vernons or Littlewoods!

A further concession was made to the Lady Subscribers in that they could now use the Red Room in the evenings after 7pm and, on Sundays after 2 o'clock for meals, but they were reminded of the now famous notice ' NO DOGS AND LADIES ALLOWED ON THE PAVILION STEPS'.

Once again the Liverpool City Council raised pecuniary matters after their adoption of the pavement in Riversdale Road, with the presentation of an account for £1,200 which was immediately opposed.

1960

Whenever the 1st team was playing an away game on the Wirral they were taken by Mr T.I.F.Tod via the New Brighton fairground where they would practice their throwing skills on the coconut shy. Such was their expertise that very soon the stall holder seeing their approach would scoop the sand out of the holders and jam in the nuts to prevent them winning. This action backfired on the fairground attendant when one of the accurate throws ricocheted back hitting a young boy between the eyes and knocking him out.

Such training proved worthwhile as both the 1st and 2nd teams enjoyed reasonable success although too many matches ended in a draw.

As table tennis was proving to be a popular 'pavilion sport' a team was started and entered the local leagues, but their success or otherwise goes unrecorded.

1961

Electricity was eventually installed in the Ladies pavilion but easy access to this facility was blocked when the club had both entrances from Beechwood Road bricked up to support their argument against paying for the adoption of the road. At last this issue was resolved with the City Council when in return for a reduction in the cost of repairs, LCC agreed not to charge an entrance fee to their ground for normal club matches.

Despite their success the Rugby Club which was attracting bigger and better opponents still only had the use of one pitch. They were not allowed use of the top ground for fear of the potential damage to the cricket pitch and so were forced to look for an alternative home. Other cricket clubs were very reluctant to lease out their grounds as most of them only had part-time groundstaff and could not accommodate Winter use. Eventually they found what they were looking for locally at St. Michaels but continued to play at Aigburth until the expiry of their five year contract. As this new venue would initially have only changing rooms but no refreshment facilities they assured LCC that they would continue to be their main base where they would re-hydrate after matches. As can be read later, this situation was not endured or enjoyed for long.

1962

A letter was received from Lancashire explaining that to hold a County game at Aigburth involved them in considerable expense for although they received 90% of the gate money nothing was paid from the proceeds of the catering or car parks. In future any such games organised be it at Liverpool, Blackpool or Southport would necessitate the payment of a fee of £350. The letter continued with the suggestion that to help meet this cost an approach be made to the Liverpool City Council.

1963

Changes were plentiful, a new President, H.H.Hughes and two new Vice Presidents, a new Secretary and a change of Steward all in the space of a few months.

The Rugby Club played their last game on the bottom field before moving to their own home ground at St.Michaels. The grandstand that they had financed was dismantled and rebuilt in situ and their new club house wall was adorned with a framed photograph of the memorial commemorating the fallen in the two World Wars. It was the end of a long association between the two clubs which had started in 1857.

Also leaving was the Gas Company who no longer had any use for the bottom ground, and as this was still superfluous to the Club's needs other than as a car park, new tenants had to be found or consideration given to selling off this asset. Fortunately either common sense or foresight prevailed and this was avoided. Liverpool Education Department became the lessees for the next five years.

The efforts of Mr T.I.F. Tod came to fruition and a welcome was given to Sefton Hockey Club who rented the top ground for their playing season at £200. With the hiring of the four tennis courts and hockey pitches during school hours by La Sagesse High School for Girls not only were the available facilities being well used the money raised was crucial to the upkeep of the Club.

Playing membership had dropped to an all time recorded low of only 150 full playing members (still only men) out of a total of 800, non-voting members i.e. House Members, Lady Subscribers or Juniors making up the difference.

Once again the club found themselves with a 'financial embarrassment' but remembering that the last appeal made to the members had failed and they could no longer depend on handouts a strict budget was drawn up allowing only £600 for any repairs and improvements in the forthcoming year.

Being the 'Swinging Sixties' members began asking for more social events and despite the financial restrictions it was decided to strengthen the floor of what was the tearoom and create a ballroom. After much discussion the maplewood floor still danced upon today was laid. Under the guidance of Mr David Bingham an Entertainments Committee was formed to orchestrate the events and it was at this time that the first gaming machine was bought. Despite breaking down in the first week due to the misuse of foreign coins a second machine was purchased for the ladies use in the Red Room.

1964

A game previously only played at colleges and military establishments was now sweeping the country and LCC felt that it should introduce this new sport to get some of the action and attract new members. This change did not come either easily or cheaply! Squash courts had to be built and although some of the longstanding members were against a disruption to their comfortable club existence, plans were drawn up for two courts. The cost was to be approximately £19,000. This would include converting the stable block into living accommodation for the Steward who up to this time lived in the main club house, thus vacating the necessary area for new changing rooms and toilets to accommodate the expected influx of both male and female players. Also advantage was to be taken of the availability of cash to redecorate the Red Room.

To meet this cost the club applied for local and government grants, brewery donations and a mortgage on the club and at last the Debentures which were issued at the beginning of the century could be redeemed, although three could not be traced.

1966

Bernard Tyler, the groundsman wishing to retire, kindly gave almost a year's notice during which time he intended to vacate The Lodge to live in a house purchased for him by his daughter, commuting daily until his departure. As a small piece of land behind this cottage had recently been sold to MANWEB for the erection of a substation the Club was confident that any Council plans to widen Riversdale Road, possibly necessitating the demolition of this corner building, would not come to fruition. They then took the opportunity to modernise and extend the premises, including a large shed and garage.

Smoking still being an acceptable pastime, the club took advantage of the sponsorship by Gallaghers to host a cricket match but unfortunately although it is believed that the event brought world class players to Aigburth no evidence of who or the result can be found.

1967

The Club was under siege! Money was available but with strings attached. The fears of the 'old school' gentlemen members were realised. Grants for the squash courts would only be available if all persons using the club had equal rights. House members, Winter Members even Lady Subscribers had to be given voting rights! Sefton Hockey Club was asked to amalgamate with LCC to form one club.

In view of the above the requirement to increase annual subscriptions by one guinea probably seemed inconsequential.

Although acceptance of the far-reaching changes had not yet been agreed work was started on the conversion of the Stable Block but was not without its problems. It was found that the building constructed in 1922 was without a damp course which only became apparent when the renovations would not dry, thus incurring further expense and delay.

1968

On the 30ᵗʰ January an Extraordinary General Meeting was convened to consider and vote on the proposed changes necessary before the building of the squash courts could commence. The resolution was easily carried, a decision that resulted in only 20 resignations from existing members but new members were now applying at a rate of the same number – per month.

A less popular decision was that to remove the 'Men Only' sign from the bar, but the sign giving rise to the title of this book was still in evidence on the pavilion steps.

To capitalize on the influx of the new breed of members 'dances' were held twice a month but as they were now taking the modern style of 'disco' concern was expressed that damage may occur in the newly furnished Red Room. To solve the anticipated problem a Disco was set up in the unused lower kitchens where the youth of the club could cavort in keeping with the style of the times.

But even in these enlightened days the Stag Evening planned for one Saturday evening was cancelled once the intended entertainment became known as it was thought to be beneath the dignity of the club.

The popularity of crown green bowls was still on the increase and a suggestion was made for a second green to be laid between the main club house and the Ladies Pavilion but as this area was in fact tennis courts resistance was strong. Winning the day for the bowlers was the offer from the Aigburth Arms, the nearby hotel, which was about to be demolished to widen Aigburth Road. They would donate their green free of charge. It was an offer not to be missed.

Once again the LCC were celebrating with the 1st XI winning the championship and the 2nd XI winning their league. It had been a long nine years.

Liverpool and District Competition 1st XI Champions 1968
Ray Tyler is front row 2nd from right

An even longer 13 years passed before success was again earned (the last to date) by the 1st XI under the captaincy of Steve Phillips in 1981.

1969

At long last the building work was complete and the Lord Mayor of Liverpool officially opened the squash courts. Within eight months 290 applications for membership had been received and accepted causing the newly appointed Squash secretary to request the committee to close the membership and start a waiting list. Heady days indeed!

1970

At 1500 members, by now only three categories - playing, non-playing and juniors, any new applicants were added to the waiting list and only those with obvious, known talent were allowed to join.

1973

Popularity for the game of squash continued to escalate and two more courts were built, almost 'on the nod' adjoining the original two built only after so much head scratching and heart-searching. Being essentially a young persons sport, the average age of the membership dropped drastically. Gone was the wealthy businessman image, those who used the club for relaxation, to be replaced by the member who found the time, energy and inclination to indulge in this frantic sport after a hard day's work.

During the winter months Thursday was the men's squash league night attracting not only the players but spectators of both sexes. As the expertise and ability improved so the matches became more of a close fought fight and on occasions a result was not obtained until after the bar closed. The players were then unable to quench their thirst. To alleviate this situation a late supper licence was applied for and granted. This resulted in refreshment being available to all members to enjoy later than usual hours allowed, making it the most popular night of the week, this despite next morning being a normal working day.

With a volume of young people using the club, some for one of the many sports now available, some just for the ambience, an extensive entertainment programme was a regular part of club life. Each of the sections seeing the opportunity not only to heighten their profile but also recognising the resulting income, some of which would come their way, vied to organize weekend events. As attendance numbers had to be restricted for safety reasons, competition for tickets was fierce and the only sure way of securing one was to offer to sell the tickets, or to be related to a seller!

The downside of this modern sport for those wishing to support either their favourite individual or cheer on their chosen team was the lack of viewing space on the balcony of the original four courts. Modern technology in the commercial world had enabled a glass backed court with spectator seating to be designed and it was felt by players and spectators alike that this innovation would greatly enhance the standing of Liverpool Cricket Club Squash Teams, attracting the better players in the county to join their ranks. A major drawback was the £53,000 required for such an enterprise whilst many of the other members of the club saw this as a takeover by the squash section to elevate their position in the club. After all it was primarily a cricket club.

Another EGM was called for and a date duly set. Whilst such meetings normally attracted a hard core of only approximately 50 people, due to the days of frantic telephone calls made by the committee stimulating interest on this occasion, it soon became evident that the Ballroom was not big enough to hold the numbers expected – either to vote for or against. It was therefore necessary to go to the expense of hiring a local school hall. On the day votes could be cast anytime during the day before the EGM and on the evening about 150 attended to hear the arguments put forward. After a stormy discussion the count of the votes revealed 211 for – 211 against. With the rules of the club leaving the casting vote with the President the motion was defeated.

The following year the resulting protracted discussions stimulated much interest and 35 people were to stand for the 10 places on the General Committee. Thirty five members who wanted to have some influence in the future direction of the club's activities.

To ease the waiting list of those wishing to join, membership was extended to 1900, a financially sound decision but one that put even more pressure on the sporting sections, particularly tennis, bowls and squash. Consequently there was a high turnover of members with 10% on average leaving each year.

Finally agreement was reached and a revised plan drawn up for the long desired glass backed court, which was built and opened in 1982. Still high demand for the most popular court times forced various pre-booking rules to be tried to make it fair for all wishing to play. For some time the booking sheet was available from 9 am seven days in advance. This changed for some the timing and/or their route to work as they would call in on the way in order to book their preferred court time. Members liked to have a set routine and play the same time each week. One well respected local GP was known to leave his patients in the waiting room on a Monday morning, albeit unaware of the reason, whilst he backtracked to the club to ensure the four courts required for himself, his wife and his friends were there for them the next week. This he did for many years until the system was changed and the start time was 8pm, resulting in a queue on site from 7.30 onwards. Such was the interest and demand for all five courts.

Squash the 'new game on the block' was now being played from 9am to 11pm every day of the week with the resulting wear and tear to the walls necessitating refurbishment every three years.

With so many people using the club, demands were made to upgrade the conditions within so an ambitious plan was drawn up to modernise the first floor of the main building. This entailed closing the entire floor for three months using instead the bar downstairs and while the regulars accepted the idea, some new members stopped coming and some older members left. When the club re-opened it continued to function as normal but financial clouds were gathering again. The renovation coincided with another major expense, the building of all weather tennis courts complete with floodlights which were desperately needed because of the amount of time lost due to adverse weather. With these, games could continue late into the evenings.

Also the rules of hockey changed. They had to play on Astro-turf but as the club did not have an artificial pitch this facility had to be hired and this proved costly indeed. To crown it all inflation throughout the country was at an all time high and club rules would only allow a 10% rise in subscriptions. The Club once again found themselves in financial difficulties.

The Liverpool Competition meanwhile continued to add new clubs to those who had been established for many years. Liverpool (1807), were of course the oldest club followed by Bootle (1833), Ormskirk (1835), Birkenhead Park (1845), New Brighton, (1857),Northern (1859), Huyton (1860) Sefton (1860) plus the now defunct Rock Ferry who had their fixtures taken over by Wallasey after World War One. Neston had been offered first team fixtures in 1909 along with Southport and Hightown in 1919. Broughton Hall, who joined in 1923 later added the prefix of Chester to their original name in 1955. In 1949 the fixtures were standardised by all clubs but there was no suggestion of a league. It was however, decided to regard the table as official.

The Liverpool Competition continued to function until 1997, when it suffered a dramatic change to its structure. Birkenhead Park, along with Chester Broughton Hall, Neston and Oxton resigned from the competition and transferred their allegiance to the Cheshire County League. To fill these vacancies the Liverpool Competition brought in Bolton and Leigh plus other clubs from Lancashire. In 1999 the competition was brought under the patronage of the English Cricket Board and a Premier league, along with a separate first division, was introduced. The tables were made out in accordance with the results of the previous season and a system of promotion and relegation was introduced. Liverpool Cricket Club was a founder member of the Premier League but unfortunately fortunes change and they were relegated to the 1st division the following year where they have remained until the present day.

CHAPTER 5

Completing the Sporting Picture

Throughout this 200 Year History of Liverpool Cricket Club only passing mention has been made of the future of this great sporting institution – the juniors. Without them there would be no club to write about today. With them all sports continue to thrive not only in the Liverpool Cricket Club but with those who for various reasons move on to other clubs, teams or areas. They take their ability to a wider field – sometimes to play against their original team mates. Thanks to the many, mostly unheralded, members giving of their time and experience to the young enthusiastic players, training and guiding not only for their chosen sport but for life.

Notable among the many successes of these youngsters is the creditable Third Place in the All England Finals for the Under 15s Team at Bournemouth in 2003, the highest position any Liverpool cricket team has achieved in a national competition. The same team having been crowned the Merseyside Knock-out Champions, the Merseyside Mid-week Champions, Echo Cup Winners, Lancashire Champions and Lancashire and Cheshire Champions.

Under 15s Team 2003 with Ryan Sidebottom who presented the trophies
In 2006 the Under 13s Team won the Lancashire Under 13s Cup

Lawn Tennis

The game of Lawn Tennis has long been favoured by certain members of the club and it has had a major influence on the development of summer sport in Liverpool. There is no evidence to support the fact that any major games were ever played at Wavertree, but the game was certainly played in Liverpool. The Racquet Club, located on Upper Parliament Street, was a major venue as was the tennis club at Waterloo. Aigburth however, soon became the centre for the sport in Liverpool.

The Northern Lawn Tennis Tournament was played bi-annually on the ground from 1884 onwards. This arrangement was shared with the Northern Tennis Club of Didsbury in Manchester. The first contest at Aigburth was played on the 14th June 1884 and it featured many of the leading players of the day from both sides of the Atlantic. Several courts were marked out on the cricket field with the finals being played in front of the Pavilion. The Ladies Singles was won by Miss Edith Davies (Claydon) who received prize money of ten guineas. She also became the holder of the Ladies Silver Challenge Trophy, valued at twenty guineas, which was donated by Liverpool Cricket Club. Mr. J B Ismay, of the Waterloo club, won the Men's Single Final while Mr Donald Stewart (West Middlesex.) won the Gentleman's Open Final. The tournament went from strength to strength as the years passed with as many as twelve pitches being required on the bottom field alone.

The Ladies Doubles Final of 1892
The player on the left is the legendary Charlotte, "Lottie" Dod

The tennis section is still very much a feature of everyday life at Aigburth. The Ladies section were, during the 1950s and 60s, considerably stronger with several of their players representing Lancashire.

The pride and joy of the section were three grass courts approached through an archway between the steward's house and the main entrance and situated between the main pavilion and the three storey brick building in the same architectural style. This was known as the Ladies' Pavilion, and had limited resources i.e. only cold running water, but it served as home to the ladies. There were also six grass and three shale courts at the bottom left of the cricket ground next to the railway. At weekends afternoon tea was served on the lawn in front of the Ladies Pavilion.

Ladies were Associate Members, not allowed to vote or allowed in the main pavilion apart from access to the 'Red Room' for drinks. This was only possible via the side steps of the pavilion.

The three top courts were lost in 1968 when the ladies of the bowling section raised enough money to make a second bowling green on the site.

In 1973 two all weather courts with floodlights were laid in the bottom right hand corner of the field. These have since been turned into additional car parking space.

The Kramer Professional Circus, during the same era, visited the Aigburth ground on several occasions and many famous players were seen on the ground. Amongst them were such household names as Lew Hoad, Ken Rosewall and Pancho Gonzalez. In the 1970s the Liverpool and District Championships were held at the club. Extra grass courts were prepared on the Riverside Road side of the ground in front of the covered grandstand. (This feature has since been removed.) The tournament was the responsibility of the club tennis members and the venue alternated between Aigburth and Birkenhead. Three tennis courts, originally made of shale, were converted to Astro-turf in 1989 and floodlights were added. This facility allows the tennis season to be extended and enables matches to be completed in inclement weather. There have even been regular "fun tournaments" on Boxing Day.

The style of tennis matches changed when both ladies and men's teams joined the Liverpool District League. Until this time the matches had been mixed friendly games. For many years the two ran side by side but a mixed friendly match is now a rarity. The club teams have won these Leagues over a number of years.

The tennis section is still very active with three men's and two ladies' teams playing in the Liverpool and District League and taking in other Lancashire club knockout tournaments.

The Ladies First Team has been constantly strong over the last fifty years, always playing in and winning Section A of the league. On occasions they have won the Lancashire Leibert competition, and currently have both county and national players in the team as well as promising juniors.

Social tennis is still played on Wednesday evenings and Saturday afternoons. In 1995 an exchange visit between veterans of LCC and Lilliental Tennis Club Bremen, Germany took place which still 'continues on a two yearly basis'.

Today the rarity of grass courts in the area means that the club hosts a number of events such as Ladies' county matches and preliminary rounds of the Liverpool International Tennis Tournament.

The Merseyside area has produced many outstanding sporting individuals but none of them can compare with the achievements and all-round ability of Lottie Dod. She was born, the daughter of a wealthy cotton broker, in Bebington on the 24th September 1871 and learned to play tennis on the private court at her home. At the early age of 14 years she joined the Waterloo Tennis Club. She first came to notice when, partnered by her sister Anne, she won the Ladies Doubles Championship at the annual tennis tournament. Next summer she entered the ladies singles contest at Wimbledon and defeated the reigning champion

Charlotte "Lottie" Dod

Blanche Bingley, in the final. She was just 15 years and 285 days old and remains to this day, the youngest person ever to win the Ladies Singles at the All England Club. Lottie Dod went on to win the Wimbledon title for the next four years before she retired from the contest. She was then instrumental in the formation of Spital Ladies Hockey club from where she captained Cheshire and was picked to play for England. Lottie then focused her attentions on the game of golf and under the watchful eye of "Thosper" Potter; she began playing at the Royal Liverpool Club. The former Liverpool cricket player helped her to perfect the skills that were required to compete at the highest level and in 1902 she won the Ladies Open Golf Championship at Troon. It was around this time that she left Merseyside and went to live in the South of England. In 1908, at the Olympic Games in London, Lottie won a Silver Medal for Great Britain in the Ladies Archery contest. Lottie Dod was an accomplished horse rider and an excellent ice skater. She was trained to concert standard on the pianoforte and possessed a powerful contralto voice. Charlotte spent the last years of her life in a nursing home at Sway on the edge of the New Forest where she died on the 27 July 1960. This exceptionally talented lady is regrettably, almost forgotten on her native Merseyside.

Quoits

Quoits is a game in which heavy metal rings are pitched or tossed underhand, at a short metal spike that is driven into the ground. The game is thought to date back to ancient Greece and the early Olympics. It is purported that quoits was brought to Britain by Roman Soldiers who played the game with the circular horseshoes discarded by their own cavalry units. The game was eventually taken up by the Ancient Britons who played it in front of the local Blacksmith's forge. (Putting the shot and throwing the hammer are also thought to have developed in the same way.) The game was later played at Inns and Taverns where the regulars formed teams and challenged each other to matches. Liverpool Cricket Club formed a team in 1890 which still survives to the present day. The side however, now plays just once a year. An annual contest, first played in 1902, is played against Childwall Quoiting Club. The Childwall club, which is the oldest in Liverpool, has been in existence since before 1800. The home fixture is played near the pavilion at Aigburth while the away fixture takes place at the Childwall Abbey Hotel.

Liverpool (Rugby) Football Club

The Liverpool Club claims to be oldest open rugby club in the World. Their first match, dated, 19th December, 1857, was played on the Liverpool Cricket Ground at Spekefields in Wavertree. Frank Mather a former pupil at Rugby School is the individual who first brought this form of football to Liverpool. Mr Mather wrote to a former school friend, Richard Sykes, and invited him to bring a side from his native Manchester to play against a team of players living in Liverpool. Mr Sykes accepted the offer and brought with him a ball that was appropriate for the occasion. Many of the Liverpool players were paid up members of Liverpool Cricket Club who, it must be assumed were looking out for a winter pastime.

There was a large fashionable crowd present and the game was played as "Rugby versus the World". The rugby players were now to form a strong link with the cricket club as the popularity at the game began to increase. They could be seen, during the winter months, playing their matches on the Spekefield ground. Cricket however, still dominated the location.

The rugby players remained at Wavertree for two years after the cricketers had left, until as the industrial development closed in, they were forced to leave. They next found a home on the ground of Sefton Cricket Club which was, at the time, situated behind the Brook House Tavern on Smithdown Road. The location, known locally as "The Brookfield's", was home to the club for two years.

The Liverpool Club then played one season on the grounds of Liverpool College at Fairfield before making overtures to rejoin their old landlords at their new home in Aigburth. The application, to play football on the new cricket field, was, for the time being, refused by the resident committee. The rugby players, not to be deterred, looked elsewhere.

They secured the piece of land that lay behind the Aigburth Hotel which was opposite the cricket club. Again they approached the cricket committee who agreed to allow them the use of their new pavilion in which to change, but only during the closed season. The after match hospitality nonetheless, would be dispensed in the Aigburth Hotel. The rugby club shared this arrangement with the recently formed Liverpool Ramblers AFC. Liverpool Football Club remained at this location for two years until the cricket club committee, at their

AGM consented to allow football to be played in front of the pavilion at a seasonal rent of £5. These arrangements were, once again, also enjoyed by Liverpool Ramblers AFC.

Extensive repairs to the cricket field next season forced the rugby players to move back across Aigburth Road and fulfil their fixtures on the former ground. Here they opened the season with an attractive fixture against the Welsh Challenge cup holders, Llanelli. The game was unfortunately played in the most adverse of weather conditions reducing the crowd to only the most dedicated followers of the sport. The match, a close run affair, ended in a victory for the Saucepan Makers from South Wales. Liverpool next crossed the Pennines where they were defeated by Bradford. The attendance, over 10,000 in number, reflected the popularity of rugby football amongst the inhabitants of the White Rose County where large crowds flocked to the major matches. This however, was not the case in Liverpool.

Over in the northern end of the City the followers of Association Football were beginning to increase in numbers. This fact was apparent when, on 27th November 1886, Bootle faced their deadly rivals Everton, in a Liverpool Cup tie. The match, played at the Bootle cricket ground on Hawthorne Road, produced a sight never before witnessed on Merseyside. Thousands of people could be seen descending on the enclosure from all directions as the kick-off time approached. The size of the crowd was estimated to be over 10,000 in number as the players took to the field. They pressed hard on the ropes that surrounded the pitch and consistently spilled onto the field of play bringing the game to a halt. Everton, with a goal in each half, won the tie 2-0. Bootle AFC, after one season in the Football League, folded in 1893 and their place was taken by the recently formed Liverpool Football Club. This title now brought them into dispute with the existing football club at

Aigburth. The Liverpool rugby players feared that two clubs with the same name might lead to some confusion. The association club, to avoid any acrimony, decided to go under the name of "Liverpool Football Club and Athletic Grounds PLC

*An entry from the Liverpool Cricket Club
minute book 1882*

After one season Liverpool (Rugby) Football Club returned to the Liverpool cricket ground and raised their posts in front of the pavilion. On 4th October 1884 they won their opening home match at the expense of Preston Grasshoppers. The Liverpool Rugby Club now had several rivals on Merseyside. Waterloo, established 1882, played at Blundellsands which were not far from the Bootle Wasps ground at Marsh Lane. Liverpool Wanderers played on Irlam Road cricket ground while the Walton Club took on their opponents at Rice Lane. New Brighton and Birkenhead Park were the leading clubs on the Wirral, and Tuebrook could be found playing on the portion of West Derby Road that lay beyond Green Lane.

The rugby section was to remain part of the scene at Aigburth for many years to come with many of the members playing cricket for the cricket club in the summer. Edward Kewley and Arthur Kemble were amongst the leading players and they represented England at both Rugby and Cricket. In 1895 Liverpool Rugby Club refused to join the breakaway Northern

Union and remained part of the Rugby Union. The Northern Union, in 1922, became the Rugby League.

The rugby players meanwhile had moved the playing pitch to the other side of the railway and on the 29th September 1899 the location was opened with a game against the Blackeley Club from Manchester. The rugby section had a last found a permanent home and an outsider's opinion of their progress was given by Capt Philip Trevor in his book, titled "Rugby Football" published in 1903.

"Liverpool is a splendid instance of a club which in spite of all temptations and discouragements has been loyal to its old traditions, and has kept the legitimate flag flying regardless of stress or form. Its president is A T Kemble, a gentleman whose name needs no introduction to good sportsmen in all parts of the land. I cannot do better than quote his remarks on the subject of an organisation for whose success he is largely responsible. He says the club is a very old one, but has not in any way deteriorated. There are more members now than ever, and we can turn out three teams every Saturday. The club has longer distances to travel now owing to the Northern Union having drawn away from former opponents, but, as a set-off the matches are far more pleasant. We now play several junior clubs, strictly amateur, and we have several local clubs to contend with who work on the same amateur lines as ourselves, viz, Birkenhead Park, Liverpool Old Boys, and others. The club is worked strictly in accordance to the rules of the Rugby Union. Members pay their own expenses.

The gates (though welcome when they exist) are a secondary consideration. Each candidate for membership has to pass the ballot in the ordinary way, and is fined for delay in the payment of subscriptions. The club has the use of the fine pavilion of the Liverpool Cricket Club for dressing accommodation, and a portion of the playing fields for their matches.

The rugby club, during their occupation of the lower ground slowly tailored the venue to suit their requirements. Extra accommodation was put in place for the standing spectators while seating was provided in the wooden grandstand. This structure was burnt down but was later replaced by one that was more substantial. R H Turner, who played for Liverpool, captained Scotland while C Lloyd, from the same team, skippered his native Ireland. It was around this time that the Chavasse twins were involved with the club along with Ronnie Poulton.

Ronald Poulton-Palmer

Ronnie Poulton was born on 12th September 1889 in Oxford. He attended Rugby Public School until, on returning to his native City, he attended Balliol College and was awarded a Rugby Blue. On leaving university he joined Liverpool Rugby Club and became their Captain. Once in Liverpool he took to the field in the same club side as R. F. Turner, and C. Lloyd He left Liverpool to become Chairman of Huntley and Palmers Biscuit Works at Reading and later played for Harlequins. Ronnie Poulton-Palmer as he now was called went on to gain seventeen caps for England and scored five tries as they won the grand slam in 1914. At the outbreak of War he enlisted in the Royal Berkshire Regiment and, on 5th May 1915 was killed at Ploegstreert Wood near Ypres.

Many members of the club who lost their lives in the First World War are recorded on the club memorial in the pavilion, many of whom were from the rugby section. This fact was illustrated when, 19th October 1919, the club fixtures resumed with a match against Waterloo. Only two of the players had previously played in the Liverpool first XV.

The players of Liverpool Rugby Club shortly before World War One.
F H Turner is seated in the centre of the middle row while
R Poulton-Palmer is seated to his right

The club slowly rebuilt their numbers while continuing to play their matches at Aigburth. In 1957, on the occasion of their centenary, they arranged a day of celebration which began with a rugby match at Aigburth. The home XV, made up of players from both Liverpool and Manchester, were opposed by a team of players from both Blackheath and Richmond. The match ended in a win for the home side by 19 points to 5. That evening, to complete the festivities, a celebration dinner was held at the Adelphi Hotel in Liverpool.

Liverpool Rugby Club eventually left the cricket club and set up home on the site of a disused golf course at St Michael's. The grandstand at Aigburth was dismantled and rebuilt on the new ground. Dressing rooms, designed by a club member, were then added to the location in a large building that also contained a refreshment lounge. The club remained at St Michael's until, plagued by vandals and lack of local interest, they amalgamated with St Helens RUFC on their ground at Moss Lane. On the 3rd May 1986 Liverpool Rugby Club played their last game at St Michael's. To-day, as Liverpool/St Helens, the club plays their matches in North 2 West Division of the rugby pyramid.

Bowls

In 1908, due to the increase in senior members, it was suggested that a bowling green be added to the enclosure. The plan was warmly received and work on this enterprise soon began. The best laid plans however, went astray. This was due to the poor quality soil use by the firm of contractors, from Chester, who were engaged to complete the task. The problem was also compounded by the excessively bad weather, The soil, it was later discovered, contained an abnormal amount of flowering weeds whose seeds, aided by the wind and rain, began to affect the once inviolable verdure of the cricket field. Troops were quickly mobilized. The committee called in a team of experts who at once ordered the soil to be removed and replaced with compound of superior quality. In 1910, amid the minimum of formal procedure, the new bowling green was opened.

The popularity of the game slowly increased and a second green was added. Sadly it was at the expense of the three tennis courts, at the east of the pavilion that had been previously used by the Ladies. The turf for the new green came from the nearby Aigburth Hotel which, due to road improvements was about to be demolished. The demise of bowling greens in public parks has led to an increase in demand on the private clubs making Aigburth one of the most popular venues in Liverpool. The bowls section still thrives today.

Hockey

Liverpool Ladies

The game of Hockey was started in England around 1880 and was designed as a closed season activity for cricket players. Hockey was the first field sport to be played by both sexes and quickly became popular throughout Victorian England. However it was the ladies who, in 1894, first brought this activity to Aigburth.

The Liverpool Ladies was one of the founder members of the England Women's Hockey Association. This governing body founded in 1896 was the first of its kind to be made up entirely of women. The founder members were based mostly in and around the Universities and Colleges in the south of England with the exception of Liverpool who was the only club situated north of Bedford.

It must be assumed, in accordance with the social restrictions of the time, that the early hockey matches at Aigburth were played by teams of players made up from the many lady subscribers of the club. They had their own facilities which enabled them to operate independently of the male members. They did however; have to pay a ground rent. Other cricket clubs, such as Hightown and Birkenhead Park quickly followed the example set by their sisters at Aigburth and formed hockey sections of their own. The game was beginning to spread throughout the North of England.

The Liverpool Ladies originally took to the field wearing a long navy skirt, a navy blouse with a stiff white collar and cuffs and a red, black and white striped tie. The whole outfit was finished off by the wearing of a straw boater.

On 5th December 1901 Liverpool Ladies lined up to face

Kersal (Manchester) with a team that included the three daughters of Rev F J Chavasse, the Bishop of Liverpool. The talents of the female members did not end on the hockey field. The Chavasse girls were amongst the female members who, at a rent of £10 a season formed a cricket team that played their matches on the lower field. The female associate members enjoyed many happy years playing their chosen sport until owing to the strict ground rules laid down by the groundsman they elected to leave their ancestral home and strike out for pastures new.

The Liverpool Ladies then began a great Odyssey.

In 1925 the Hockey players began playing at Deysbrook Lane before moving to Crawfords Sports Club where they remained till 1951. They next moved to the grounds of the Old Hall at Sandfield Park. The owner of the property, Mrs. Thompson-Smith, was the President of the club at the time. This generous lady, at her own expense, laid out a new pitch which was maintained by her own personal chauffeur. Liverpool Ladies remained there until 1981 when Mrs. Thompson-Smith passed away. The club, following the sale of their ground then found a base at Wavertree Cricket Club where they remained for three years. In 1983, following the advent of Astroturf, the team began playing at the sports centre on Picton Road and used Sefton Cricket Club as their base. In 1989 the club played on the grounds of Liverpool University before amalgamating with their hosts to become, as they are to-day, Liverpool Sefton Ladies H C.

Throughout the years, the Liverpool Ladies have provided players at both County and International level. Clare Owens has captained Wales while Pat Park, Rita Bentley, June Birrall, Lorna Clark and Maureen Short have all played for England. Martha Rigg has captained Lancashire while many other players, too numerous to mention, have also represented the Red Rose County.

On 3rd March, 1979 the Aigburth ground hosted a Ladies International Hockey match between England and Wales. The Lord Lieutenant of Merseyside, Brigadier Sir Douglas Crawford C.B., D. F. O.,T.D. was on hand to greet the teams in front of a large and colourful crowd that consisted mainly of schoolgirls. The Welsh, following the bully off, pressed their opponents and the home sides were grateful to a goal line clearance from Mary Eckersall of Ormskirk. England however slowly got the upper hand and goals from Gordon and Swinnerton gave them a 2-0 victory.

Modern day railway trains, to and from London, today glide, quietly past the present home of Liverpool Ladies The neatly laid out playing pitch, made of Astroturf, is contained within the grounds of the Liverpool College. The setting is dominated by a newly built sports hall in which the players change. The club currently plays in the Women's National League North Division which takes them to play as far away as Nottingham, Whitley Bay and Durham. The Liverpool Sefton Ladies, after their home matches, entertain the visiting sides back at their original home in the pavilion of the Liverpool Cricket Club at Aigburth. The ankle length skirts, along with the striped ties and straw boaters, have long since disappeared as the players take to the field wearing the relaxed style of the day. Nevertheless, navy blue still remains the club colour.

Liverpool / Sefton Ladies Hockey Team, 2006/2007

Liverpool / Sefton Men's Hockey Club

The present day male hockey players have a history that is not dissimilar to that of the female players. Beginning life, in 1885, as the Blantyre Recreation Club, they began by playing their home matches behind the Brook House Hotel on Smithdown Road. John Kendall, a Colour-Sergeant of the 2nd Volunteer Battalion, The Kings (Liverpool) Regiment, and a few fellow Volunteers of his Regiment formed a club with the intention of playing hockey and rounders. In 1889, following a change of venue, the team became known as Sefton Hockey Club. When, in the same year, the Lancashire County Hockey Association was formed, Sefton became one of the first clubs to be affiliated to the society. The other clubs, who helped found the Association, are now defunct thus leaving Sefton as the oldest male hockey club in the North of England.

The team, during their formative years, formed a close bond with the South Manchester club both on and off the field. The teams played regular fixtures and at alternate venues an annual dinner dance was held after the match. These events continued until the demise of the Manchester club.

The venue at Aigburth, with its excellent playing surface, has always proved popular with the sports governing body and the ground has staged many important matches at both county and international level. On the 26th March 1966 the ground was selected to host a male International hockey match between England and Wales. There were, owing to the proximity of the Principality, many Welsh supporters in the "good crowd" that gathered to witness the event. The match was played in a swirling wind. England, with goals from Barham (2) and Knight, won the game 3-0. In 1972 a second international match was played on the ground. England, this time playing host to Ireland, won the game 2-0.

The first member of the club to gain honours was T. Fitz Porter who played for Lancashire and the North in 1892 as did A. W. Brock, a fine goalkeeper, in 1905. In 1895 Idris R. Jones was selected as centre-half for Wales in their first international match.

Three members playing at their best around the turn of the century were G.C. Dawson (1895) C. Simpson and R. W. McCay (1907). All took a very prominent part in the life of the Club, all were first team Captains and played for Lancashire.

Charles Simpson was a member of the Lancashire Selection Committee and devoted about 40 years to the club and particularly to hockey. In 1910, M. L.Pool was selected for the county and the following year played in goal in all the games for Lancashire and the North of England, receiving his cap.

Sefton has never owned a ground and has, therefore, been subject to the whims of others and, in consequence, has moved about Liverpool all too often.

The first known ground was a field at the back of the Brook House Hotel, perhaps called "Woodcroft". Later a pitch was in use in Sefton Park, Mossley Hill Drive, but for many years after that, the club had the use of the Wavertree Recreation Club's ground in Sandown Lane. The Club had to leave around 1910 as the Cricket Club wanted to eradicate the plantain in the turf.

From here, the Club moved to Huyton Cricket Club but the lease terminated shortly after. This ground known to many Sefton players has an attractive setting and is very true and pleasant to play on. Immediately following the First World War, the club was unable to obtain a satisfactory ground although some games were played on a pitch in Broadgreen. After a brief spell back at Huyton, the club once again had to seek a ground and was successful in obtaining the use of a pitch, if it may be called that, at Tuebrook Villa, Green Lane, Stoneycroft. It was with considerable relief to the club and to its opponents that in 1932, the Huyton Cricket Club again allowed the use of their ground. Following the Second World War, Huyton were unfortunately unable to let the Club have the ground again owing to its need for attention. However, permission was granted to use the ground of the Liverpool Cricket Club at Aigburth, which lasted only one season. More negotiation followed and the Club returned to Huyton. It can be said that Sefton Hockey Club has had more than its fair share of difficulties, but in spite of that, it has continued throughout to play its part in the game of hockey in Lancashire.

The Sefton Hockey Club moved to Aigburth and became Liverpool Sefton Hockey Club in 1963. The first game was home to Sale on the 5th October 1963. The improvement in facilities as a consequence of this move resulted in an influx of good new players and increased the status of the club.

England v Wales at Aigburth 1966

The Cricket Club has hosted many prestigious events over the years.

These were in the days when hockey was still played on grass. The advent of Astroturf changed this. The advantage of having the best playing surface in the North of England for drawing representative matches to the Club was lost. In those days the grass playing surface at the Club was superb. Quotes: "Like a bowling green". "How are we expected to play hockey on a perfect surface like that" are from one of the Irish players playing against England and said in jest! It was also of great advantage financially and socially to the Cricket Club as it transformed it into an all year round active organization rather than one that could not be used in winter.

Boxing Day Matches were traditional matches played between Lancashire and Cheshire each year. They were very well attended by most of the players in Lancashire and Cheshire. It was always a festive occasion and Liverpool Cricket Club managed to stage many of the Lancashire home games. These games were a good source of revenue on the day and a great advert for the facilities.

In the early nineties there were the Veteran's Tournaments and although playing a much lower standard of hockey ensured that the Cricket Club was full of people enjoying themselves. Eleven men's and six women's teams took part in these tournaments travelling from as far afield as Holland, Germany, Ulster, The Republic of Ireland and Scotland to enjoy the festive hockey. Hockey, marquees, dinners and speeches, were good revenue for the Club and a wonderful use of the facilities. They were notable for the fact that many members from other sections of the Club used to look forward to them and enjoy the festive singing and dancing.

At this time there were seven senior sides and a Badgers's team playing most Saturdays as well as Sunday friendly fixtures and Veterans games.

During this golden period of the seventies, eighties and early nineties the 1st' team were winners of the Lancashire Club Championship: 1975-76, 1983-84 and 1987-88, and qualified for the Northern Counties Knock-out Cup, which the team won in 1976, becoming Knock-out Champions of the North of England. The Club won the North West League in 1974-75 qualifying for the All England Finals in Birmingham, then also the North West League in 1977/78 qualifying for the all England finals in Aldershot. In 1985/86 the team again won the North West League.

The Club were also winning all day local tournaments like Winnington Park, Hightown, and Southport, and getting through several rounds in Indoor Hockey National Cups.

The team had 5 current players in a successful Lancashire side on more than one occasion.

When the National League was first formed in 1987 the 1st team only needed to draw either of the last 2 qualifying games (played the same day) to enter the 2nd Division of the National League. A win or 2 draws would have taken them into the 1st Division. The team lost both games narrowly. Had the team been successful there would have been a great influx of new players and the following years would have been very different. But the game of hockey was now being played on Astroturf and the clubs with there own facilities were the ones to prosper and draw players of representative quality into their teams. There followed a period of steady decline and dropping down the leagues.

The Hockey section is now improving each season. The first team, led by Peter Tod, a demonstration of the continuity of involvement of the traditional Liverpool families, has gained promotion in 2004-5 and 2005-6 seasons. In 2006 they also won the National Plate Competition. This has attracted more good players and hopefully will raise the standard throughout the section to the level of the Club's outstanding years.

Among the players who achieved representative recognition during this time were: David Blackmore who joined Sefton while at school. He played a few years at Huyton Cricket Club and then moved to Liverpool Cricket Club in the early sixties.

He played for Lancashire a record 162 times over a period of 21 years dropping himself at the age of 42 as he was also a Lancashire selector. In that period Lancashire won the County Championship three times (runners up 3 times). David captained Lancashire in the last of these wins.

He played many years for the North of England, played 32 games for England, and 17 times for Great Britain. He was in the Great Britain squad when they narrowly missed qualifying for the Montreal Olympics.

He played many enjoyable and rewarding years for the Badger's team in his mid forties to mid fifties, and is now in his 5th year with the 3rd team - having been captain for 3 of those years. David also ran the Veterans Hockey team for a number of years. The veterans teams played much good hockey, with a mixture of very good and not so good players, but were a joy to play for and were especially appreciated by those who liked to get the game over with early on Sundays to leave the afternoon and evening free to socialize over a nice meal and an occasional glass or two.

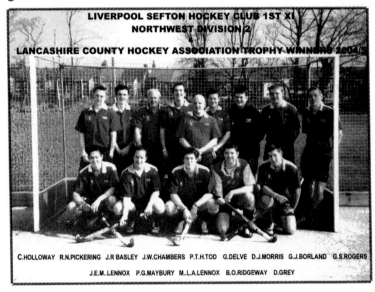

LIVERPOOL SEFTON HOCKEY CLUB 1ST XI
NORTHWEST DIVISION 2
LANCASHIRE COUNTY HOCKEY ASSOCIATION TROPHY WINNERS 2004/5

C.HOLLOWAY R.N.PICKERING J.R BASLEY J.W.CHAMBERS P.T.H.TOD G.DELVE D.J.MORRIS G.J.BORLAND G.S.ROGERS

J.E.M.LENNOX P.G.MAYBURY M..L.A.LENNOX B.O.RIDGEWAY D.GREY

David has recently played for the north over 60's team at Cannock in the Master's Tournament and for England Over 60's team at Bowdon v North Wales.

David Badley who joined Sefton from West Derby, played for Lancashire 127 times, a regular for the North of England and played 5 times for England, suffered from back problems forcing him to give up hockey and turn to golf.

John Badly (no relation) who joined Sefton from West Derby, played for Lancashire 49 times, and also for North of England was invited to an England training weekend but was unlucky not to get selected.

Steve Eyre, who joined Sefton from Sheffield University, played for Lancashire 83 times, played for the North of England, and was a regular member of the England Indoor Hockey team.

Lots of other players over the years have played representative hockey at various levels including County representation, but not with such consistency.

Liverpool Collegiate Old Boys RUFC

The Rugby code returned to Aigburth in 1999 when the Liverpool Collegiate Old Boys RUFC amalgamated with the cricket club to play on the lower ground.

They took over the ground floor of the pavilion and marked out two pitches on the lower field. Their opening match, watched by a fairly large crowd, was against Chorley in the Lancashire Cup. The Club have, in their history produced several noteworthy players. Tom, "Bully" Ellis was the first of their players to win a Lancashire Cap while Barry Smith, several years later, played for the Three Counties.

Pete Best, the former drummer with Beatles attended the Collegiate, and, with a generous donation helped to improve the floodlighting that is used during the training sessions. Today Liverpool Collegiate play their matches in Euromax South Lancs/Cheshire 3. The league, part of the National pyramid, takes them to such places as Holmes Chapel and the Isle of Man.

Liverpool Collegiate RUFC

Perhaps the most important benefit to the Rugby Section's move to Liverpool Cricket Club was the opportunity to run mini and youth rugby teams. On Wednesday 26th November 1998 more than 200 pupils from eight schools took part in a 'Rugby Taster Day' organized by the club with the help of the Rugby Youth Development Officer. Liverpool Live Cable TV Channel covered the event and produced a 15 minute programme. The resulting interest greatly boosted the number of youngsters turning up on Sunday mornings for the mini and youth sessions.

The 2004 - 05 season was one of the most successful in the history of the Club, mainly due to the success of the mini and junior section when they were honoured with a series of awards including the Lancashire Junior and Mini Rugby Club of the Year Award and the Liverpool Club of the Year Award.

The Club also received the R.F.U. Seal of Approval and the Sports England Club Mark.

During the same year the Club was delighted to display the

Rugby World Cup for a day as part of the Sweet Chariot Tour, the only club in Liverpool to be so honoured.

Several members are singled out for mention. Adam Anderson was selected to play for Lancashire Under-15s and made the North of England Squad whilst Karl Anderson played for the Royal Navy and Combined Services Under-21s at Twickenham.

The 2005 – 06 season was the 80th anniversary of the founding of the Club, an occasion marked by several events. It was during this season that saw the creation of the Collegiate Ladies XV. Their first game against Liverpool University saw them romp to a 19 – 0 victory. They are now in the Lancashire League.

Liverpool Collegiate RUFC Ladies Section

Another notable event was the presentation to one of the club's Under 10s, Jonathan Davidson when he was crowned the National Kick, Pass & Run Champion on the hallowed turf at Twickenham at the Guinness Premiership Final in May 2006. He received his award from England's most capped international Jason Leonard.

The Club now run 10 teams from under 7s to under 16s inclusive and also two colts teams.

Lacrosse

2006 saw Liverpool Cricket Club welcome Liverpool Ladies Lacrosse team and wish them a long and happy stay. During the 1980s Aigburth hosted several international women's lacrosse matches, the major one being the match between USA and England, England winning in the dying minutes.

CHAPTER 6

Aigburth today

In 1984, during the Liverpool Garden Festival celebrations, Lancashire took on the powerful West Indian touring side at Aigburth. The location, to accommodate the large all ticket attendance, was greatly enhanced with banks of temporary seating. The spectators, who numbered 8,000, were treated to possibly one of the finest exhibitions of one day batting ever seen during an International cricket match in England. It came from the West Indian opener, Gordon Greenidge.

The Barbados born player quickly lost his opening partner Desmond Haynes, who was quickly followed back to pavilion by Richie Richardson. Larry Gomes then joined Greenidge at the crease and the two players then set about the Lancashire bowling. Greenidge reached his century before Gomes, with his score on 87, was caught and bowled by John Abrahams. Greenidge however, was still looking most likely to become the first player to hit a double century in a limited over match in England. Sadly he lost the strike for long intervals during the remainder of the West Indian innings. Gordon Greenidge, from a final total of 297, scored 186 runs without the loss of his wicket. The Aigburth crowd cheered him all the way up the steps of the pavilion.

The crowd then witnessed another fine innings from Graham Fowler. The left hander stood up to the fearsome West Indian bowling attack with great courage but his efforts were not enough to save his side from defeat. The Accrington born player scored 94 before being caught by Greenidge off the bowling of Gladstone Small. A late partnership by Jack Simmons and Matthew Maynard, gave Lancashire a brief hope of victory but they eventually lost the game by 56 runs.

During the post war years the social climate at Aigburth had undergone many changes concerning the attitude towards the lady members. The famous sign on the front steps of the pavilion, still remembered by many members today, 'NO DOGS AND LADIES ALLOWED' was finally removed in the 1970s - although it should be recorded that whilst Lancashire were playing at Aigburth the balcony still remained 'off limits' to lady members until the latter years of the first millennium.

Benefit matches for several Lancashire players, have taken place at Aigburth. Brian Statham and Jack Simmons have been honoured in this manner along with Graham Fowler.

In September 1989 there occurred an international match at Aigburth between players selected from India and Pakistan. The match, owing to certain difficulties with the organisers, was put in jeopardy and only sanctioned at the eleventh hour. The caterers then began to mobilize. A convoy of pantechnicons resembling a herd of elephants left West Yorkshire at first light and began to lumber across the Pennines in the direction of Liverpool. Similar activity was also reported in the Midlands. An early morning mist, brought on by the stillness of the air, shrouded the location as all parties converged on the cricket ground and occupied the car park. Large cylinders of propane were speedily connected to gas cooking rings, tables were set up, and meals prepared. The main car park rapidly took on an atmosphere comparable to the famous Eden Gardens cricket ground in Calcutta The setting, when the morning reached its pride, became bathed in bright sunshine. The air around the enclosure was soon filled with the fragrance of the spices that make up the exotic aroma of Asian cooking. The spectators, who came mostly from east Lancashire, Yorkshire, and the Midlands then began to arrive by coach. They flooded in to the ground and encircled the playing field in great numbers. (The attendance was estimated at being around 2,000.) The players, following a short delay, then left the pavilion and took up their positions on the field.

The side representing India was captained by Mohammad Azharuddin while the Pakistan side, which included both Waqar Younis and Wasim Akram was captained by Javed Miandad. The morning play went smoothly but there was, unbeknown to the players, a certain amount of anxiety in the pavilion regarding the provision of refreshments that would meet with their approval. Monica Harford, the wife of the Club Steward, decided to approach the owner of a nearby Indian restaurant. The proprietor, who lent a sympathetic ear, assured the good lady he could, in the short time available, supply the demands of hospitality. The rest of the day went with ease and, after an entertaining days cricket, India won the match by 9 wickets. The crowd then dispersed peacefully. The caterers cleaned up the ground and left not a trace of their occupation. The Aigburth ground as the last vehicle departed was left as pristine as it was found. The day was voted a great success.

Due to the discovery of a certain diary Liverpool Cricket Club became a focal point of media attention in 1992. Michael Barrett, a local scrap dealer, claimed to have discovered evidence that a former member of the club was in fact the serial killer known as 'Jack the Ripper'. It was claimed the journal had been written by none other than James Maybrick. Mr. Barrett claimed to have been given the chronicle by a friend shortly before his death. The discovery caused a stir amongst Ripperologists on both sides of the Atlantic who were divided on their opinions as to its authenticity. The diary, denounced by local historians, is thought to be an elaborate hoax. It is still, however, the subject of much debate and has yet to be totally dismissed as a forgery.

In the same year, due to financial pressures, the club was forced to sell off one of its most valuable assets, its precious anthology of cricket books. The collection, which contained a complete set of Wisden's Annuals, also boasted many volumes of Fredrick Lilywhites Cricket scores dating back to 1746. They were bought by a local collector for an undisclosed fee.

Liverpool Cricket Ground

At the start of the new Millennium the present members of Liverpool Cricket Club are vastly different from that of their founders. The leading commercial families of Liverpool have long since disappeared to be replaced by much younger people who want to play an active part in the sport of their choice. The position of President is now bestowed upon a member who has over the years given good service to the club, while the new post of Chairman introduced in 1989 gives a more modern outlook to the management.

The Club, it was eventually discovered, could not survive solely on profits from the bar and the subscriptions of the members, so radical changes had to be made. It was decided the pavilion should be hired out for use by the general public for such functions as weddings, funerals and birthday parties. This action was frowned upon by many of the senior members but as 'needs must', the plan went ahead. The car park was also used for car boot sales but the most ambitious project to date has been the Pop Concert that took place in 2002. To protect the renowned ground from being damaged it was covered by a giant carpet. Even with pre-purchased tickets the fans started to queue at 8am and when the gates were at last opened, they stretched for over two miles. The number of people who attended the event counted over twenty thousand.

The concert was a great success with such solo artists as Ronan Keating and Will Young being seen on stage along with the SugaBabes vocal group. Finishing promptly at 9pm an army of cleaners descended on the enclosure and carted away the vast amount of rubbish that had been left by the fans. Two hours later, the ground was back to normal. The West Indian touring side played a game at Aigburth three days later and complimented the ground staff for producing an excellent wicket.

In 2003 the Club was approached by a television company who wished to 'locate' to their ground for filming an episode of the 'Forsythe Saga' using the pavilion as the backdrop to a fictional cricket match. The contest, according to the script, was the annual Eton v Harrow public school match that takes place at Lords Cricket Ground in London. The scene, enhanced by period costume, brought the long lost splendour of the 1920s back to the Aigburth enclosure. Damian Lewis, Gina McKee, and local actress Gillian Kearney played leading roles while many of the club members were to be seen as film extras at the eventual screening.

Some of the members as extras at the filming
of the Forsythe Saga at Aigburth

Liverpool Cricket Club has, over the last two hundred years, undergone many changes both on and off the field. The players of old, who first met on Mosslake Fields, would be amazed at the changes that now affect the game they once loved. It has developed from a hobby, for a few well appointed gentlemen, into a global activity that is now watched by a television audience of millions. They would however, be pleased to know that the club they formed in 1807 is still alive and thriving.

Liverpool Cricket Club, thanks to the diligence of the membership, has withstood the test of time. May the next two hundred years be as creative and continue to add to the culture of the City.

AUTHORS' NOTE

Reading through the Club minutes and newspaper reports of the last two hundred years we have 'seen' people join the club as youngsters, grow, assume positions of power, become elder statesmen and sadly die. We feel as if we have known them personally and trust that any descendants reading this account feel that we have treated them with the respect and compassion they deserve.

PRESIDENTS

1881-1897	THE EARL OF SEFTON
1898-1900	C. LANGTON
1901-1913	H. H. HORNBY
1914-1915	D. CUNNINGHAM
1916-1921	E. C. HORNBY
1922-1923	H. B. PARR
1924-1931	A. L. MELLY
1932-1934	W. B. STODDART
1935-1936	W. BATESON
1937-1955	C. S. HANNAY
1956-1961	T. B. TOD
1962	G. H. CHAMBERLAIN
1963-1967	H. H. HUGHES
1968-1971	A. E. HUSBAND
1972-1985	J. BENNETT
1986-1989	D. H. TOD
1989-1992	R. TYLER
1992	H. KING
1993-1995	A. V. NEWTON
1995-1996	K. R. JONES
1997-1998	A. G. CONNOLLY
1999-2000	K. SMITH
2001-2002	H. G. SPICER
2003-2004	J. P. MITCHELL
2005- 2007	E. WARD

CHAIRMEN

1989-1990	K. R. JONES
1991-1993	N. PYNE
1993-	P. McEVOY